Getting Behind the Wheel

What every driver should know

By R.H. Rademacher

Published By:
Pigeon River Publishing, LLC
P.O. Box 187, Haslett, Michigan 48840

www.gettingbehindthewheel.com
www.facebook.com/rhrademacher

Copyright © 2017 by R.H. Rademacher
All rights reserved. This book or any portion thereof may not be reproduced or used in any manner whatsoever without the express written permission of the publisher except for the use of brief quotations in a book review.

Printed in the United States of America

First Printing, 2017

ISBN 978-0-9991420-0-4

To my sons, John and Bobby: continue to do what you love and follow your dreams.

Table of Contents

Table of Contents	**4**
Preface	**10**
Introduction	**12**
Chapter 1: Safety First	**16**
Insurance: Your Responsibility to You and Your Fellow Drivers	*16*
Set up Roadside Assistance in Your Phone's Directory	*18*
Don't Become a Statistic	*20*
That Text Can Wait!	*20*
The Need for Speed	*21*
EPSL: Exceeding the Posted Speed Limit	*22*
DTFFC: Driving Too Fast for Conditions	*23*
"I'm Okay; I've Only Had a Couple of Drinks"	*25*
Topics with Purpose	*26*
Keep Your Hands on the Wheel, Getting Pulled Over	*27*
Chapter 2: So You Want to Buy a Car	**30**
Buy with Purpose	*31*
Size Matters	*32*

When and Where to Start Looking	34
Put Them to the Test and Then Buy From the Best	36
Buy Here, Pay Here	38
New vs. Used: The Pros and Cons	40
Avoid the Rental Return	41
If Unsure, Start Here . . .	42
Certified Pre-Owned or Used?	44
Domestic, Asian and European: What's the Difference?	44
Domestic and Asian Makes	46
Get a Pre-purchase Inspection, NOT Post Purchase!	47
The Test Drive: What to Look and Listen For	49
Thinking About Leasing a Car?	52
New Car Warranties	53
Aftermarket Warranties: Read the Fine Print	54

Chapter 3: First Things First, Before You Get Behind the Wheel — 57

Yes, We Still Need Emergency Kits	57
Where's Your Owner's Manual?	58
What's Under the Hood?	59
Check the Oil, Check the Oil, Check the Oil . . .	60
Keeping an Eye on Your Fluids: It's Easier Than You Think!	61
A Quick Look at Car Rentals—What?	63

Chapter 4: Routine Maintenance — 65

Get the Most Out of Your Purchase	65
Fueling Up: Does It Really Make a Difference?	65

Lube, Oil & Filter: Same Thing, Only Different	68
Belts and Hoses	70
Don't Forget About the Blades	71
Tires Work Great Under Pressure: Keep Them Inflated and Rotated	72
Stop!	74
Shocks, Struts and Other Suspension Stuff	76
Tires, Brakes and Suspension All Work Together As a Team . . .	78
Do I Really Need a "Tune-up"?	79
80,000 to 100,000 Miles: The Ever-important Timing Belt	80
Throttle Body What?	81
Cleaning Fuel Injectors?	83
Cooling System Flush or Exchange	83
Transmission Fluid	85
Brake and Power Steering Fluid Service: Hmmm . . .	86
A/C Service: Some Like It Hot	86
Don't Forget the Filters	89
Cabin Air Filter	90
Is Your Car Ready for That Long Trip? Get a Pre-trip Inspection	91
Moving On . . .	92
Chapter 5: Car Problems? Things You Should Know.	**94**
Breaking Down	94
Now, What's Your Car Doing?	95
What's It Not Doing?	96
Look and Listen to What Your Car Is Telling You	101
"There's a Light on! What's Wrong With My Car?"	103

Purchase a Scan Tool, Because Knowledge Is Power	104
BlueDriver Scan Tool for iPad, iPhone and Android Smart Phones	106
P0440 to P0449: Evaporative Emissions Codes	108
P0562: Low System Voltage	109
P0128: Thermostat Below Regulated Temperature	109
P0300 to P0312: Misfire Codes	110
P0420 to P0434: Catalyst Efficiency Below Threshold	111
P0130 to P0167: Oxygen Sensor Failures	112
P0100 to P0109: MAF and MAP Sensor Codes	114
P0171 and P0174: Lean Code	115
There Won't Be a Test on This Later	116
What Diagnostic Trouble Codes Are and What They Aren't	117
The No-code Condition	118
A Word About Reprogramming (Re-flashing)	119
Are You Your Car's Best Friend or Worst Enemy?	120
Rodents Belong Out in the Wild, not Under Your Hood	121
It's Not a Speed Boat	123
Small Keepsakes, Big Problems	124
Pop, Soda, Coke . . .	126
Secure That Cargo!	127
Chapter 6: Choosing a Repair Shop and Technician, What to Look For	**129**
Where to Look	130
You've Found Your Auto Repair Shop, Now What?	134
Identifix or iATN	134
Ask to See the Shop	135

Hire a Technician, Not a Mechanic	136
Can't We All Just Get Along?	138
If Your Tech is Great, Throw Them a Bone	140
Parents of College Students, Listen Up!	141
Now, Let's Get Your Car Repaired	143
Chapter 7: Getting Your Vehicle Repaired – What Should You Expect?	**144**
First, the "Write Up"	144
The Estimate	145
Something for Nothing	147
Breaking Down the Parts of Your Estimate and Invoice	148
Parts Are Parts, Right?	149
"We Don't Install Customer-supplied Parts"	153
Labor	154
Apples to Apples	155
"I Didn't Build It, I Didn't Buy It and I Didn't Break It"	158
Know Your Rights	158
Don't Keep Paying for the "Same" Repair	160
Patience Is a Virtue	161
What About Insurance Related Repairs?	163
Time to Pick Up Your Ride	164
Conclusion	**166**
What's that Mean?	**168**
Drivability Symptoms	168
Brakes and Exhaust Symptoms	170

| What Every Driver Should Know | 9 |

Wheels and Suspension Symptoms   *171*

Websites to Remember   **174**

Preface

Years ago, when I bought my first car, a 1972 VW Super Beetle, I was clueless on what was required to maintain it. The first time my car broke down, I was on a weekend road trip driving from Norfolk, Virginia to a small town in Pennsylvania with my girlfriend. As we were cruising up U.S. Highway 13, probably listening to a local oldies station on the radio, my Beetle began to misfire and jerk violently. It didn't matter how much gas I gave her, she just wouldn't go or run any better. I had no idea what was wrong; I just prayed that it would keep running and make it to the next exit. This was before cell phones, so it meant walking or hitch-hiking to the next town if necessary. At that moment I thought to myself, what a way to impress my girlfriend, who was about to meet some of my family in Pennsylvania. Fortunately, I was able to limp my car along until we got to that next exit, where there was a service station that was able to get us in right away.

A lot has changed since the early '80s; many advances in automotive technology have made automobiles more reliable and able to keep running longer. It's not surprising to see, with the proper care, vehicles still on the road with 150,000 or more miles on the odometer. Nevertheless, it takes regular preventative maintenance and staying on top of any repairs that come along. In addition, vehicle owners are more informed than they used to be. With the advent of the internet and smart phones, information is at your fingertips. This makes it easier to look up prior maintenance schedules, find good repair facilities, and even get help when the need arises.

On the other hand, I've seen a greater need for a book that will serve as sort of a guide in the purchasing, driving and maintaining of today's highly advanced cars and trucks. On a weekly basis, I see customers come to me in a state of bewilderment, not knowing whether they should keep their aging car or truck, or if they should trade it in because of the cost of a repair. I've seen patrons, on the brink of tears, pleading with me to fix the light on the dash, which turned on while they were driving on a trip.

Don't be dismayed, there is hope! With this book as your guide, you can wade through the confusion and the advertising rhetoric. You will be able to figure out just what type of vehicle you would like to purchase, maybe even right down to the make and model. You will be able to confidently navigate the automotive repair scene and find that qualified shop or technician that will become a long-lasting relationship. You will know what to do if a light on your dash comes on, or your car stalls out while you're driving on a trip or to a vacation destination. Owning and driving an automobile should not be a stressful low point in your life; it should be an exciting highlight, maybe even exhilarating!

Introduction

This book is a record of years of my personal experiences, as an owner, driver, ASE certified technician and repair shop owner. I will also refer to some experiences of others, both drivers and technicians. I have been working on vehicles for more than thirty years, though I will be the first to tell all of you that I am not the final authority on everything there is to know about the automotive industry or repair. If you gather up ten technicians and asked them all the same questions concerning which vehicles are the best, or how to perform this or that service, you will most likely get ten different answers. Are all of them right or are they all wrong? Probably neither—they are an accumulation of their experiences as well. Nevertheless, one theme will be common: performing the routine maintenances at regular intervals.

One experience I encountered as a young technician, and I will never forget this, was working at a Marathon service station when a young college student had her car towed to the shop. The car had quit running while she was driving it. It didn't take long for us in the shop to find out what had happened. As usual, we did the basic checks first: check the antifreeze, also referred to as coolant in the repair business. When we checked the oil, we found that there was no oil on the dipstick (not a good sign). At that point, we removed the oil drain plug, and about two or three cups of what looked like a very black tarry remnant of what used to be oil, the lifeblood of the engine, dripped out of the oil pan. We checked to see if the engine was damaged, due to the lack of oil; after removing the valve cover, we discovered that the camshaft was seized and would not turn. This surprised us, because the engine was only about eighteen months old. After asking the young customer when last she'd had her oil changed, she just gave us a perplexed look. After digging a little deeper, we had found out that when she bought the car brand new, the dealership had never told her about the routine maintenance that was required. They took her money and sent her on her way. She had no idea that she had to get her oil changed occasionally or even checked—general car maintenance was never explained to her. Away from home and away from her family, she was devastated. Imagine being the technician telling the girl that the car that she had just purchased a little over a year ago needed some major engine work done or the engine replaced.

There is a reason why I shared this experience with you, the reader. The purpose why I set out to write this book is to help educate you in any way that I can. There is some misinformation out there, and the good information that is available can be hard to find. Had this young lady been properly taught, or given the needed information to maintain her car, she would have continued on with her day, instead of having to call a tow truck. Okay, as mentioned earlier, perhaps other techs may disagree on what brand of oil is the best. However, it doesn't really matter if the oil never gets changed, does it?

When I owned and operated my repair shop in Ohio, I made it a point to educate my customers. On a regular basis, I would tell them that it didn't matter if my shop did the work or not. If I thought a certain repair, maintenance, or procedure needed to be completed on their car, I would tell them, whether I got the job or not. Sounds pretty insane, huh? My customers always appreciated that. When I was willing to send them away, perhaps to another shop, they knew I was being straight up with them. No high-pressured sales to get them into my shop for repairs that they weren't comfortable doing at that point in time.

I treat my customers as I would want a shop or technician to treat one of my family members if they were away from home and in an unfamiliar city looking for help. I am blessed to have two sons and three stepsons. As of the writing of this book, three of them have their driver's licenses and two of them will soon be on the path to getting their drivers permits. They all have their own strengths and weaknesses when it comes to driving and car ownership. Yes, they are all young, but I see many of these same tendencies in seasoned adult drivers. My oldest son John, when it came to driving, was very nervous, and he still is to some extent. He's very methodical and has no problem checking the oil or what's necessary. He has the mechanical skills to take care of what he drives. On the other hand, he really doesn't enjoy driving, partly because of fear of what could happen while he's behind the wheel. In his mind, it's a "necessary evil." My oldest stepson Corbin, on the other hand, is a natural behind the wheel: it's as if he was born with a steering wheel in his hands. On the down side, we have to remind him constantly to check the coolant, top off the oil, etc.

John and Corbin, two different drivers with their own strengths and weaknesses when it comes to driving; and so it is with most of the populace, except for the few car buffs that are extremely skilled in both. In addition, of course there are a few that are very nervous drivers, that my stepmother used to call "Nervous Nellies," who knew very little about cars or how to drive them. This book is an important guide for all of these groups.

Once you have finished reading this book I would like you to go out and put it out in the glove box or storage compartment of your vehicle. Now this may sound strange, but the reason I mention this is that I would like you to be prepared if ever you should need to quickly look up some information. When you are ready to buy a car, there is a section on that. When you need to find a good repair shop or technician, there's a section on that. If your car is acting up or a warning light comes on, there's a section on that as well.

This book is for everyone, young or old, male or female. It doesn't matter what income bracket you're in or whether you are driving a Chevrolet or a Mercedes-Benz. The questions I've been asked, the situations I've witnessed have crossed all boundaries. So to all of you out there, and I know some of you, who have told your technician, "I don't know anything about cars...," this book is for you. After reading this, you will!

Chapter 1 may seem rather rudimentary but I felt that it should be included to help some of the younger or less experienced drivers out there. It may seem basic but it is just as important as all the other chapters. Because this book is geared (pardon the pun) towards all drivers, it is important to cover the basics before the reader, or perhaps your son or daughter, starts getting behind the wheel.

Okay, so let's get started.

Chapter 1: Safety First

Whether you are younger or older, it can be daunting to think about all that is required for that card or piece of paper that says you've earned the privilege to drive. Remember, driving is a privilege, not a right; so what now? I'm not going to dwell on what was probably taught to you during driver's training, but I will hit on a few highlights. This chapter will cover some fundamental aspects of driving for the new driver, and not get into the actual vehicle aspect yet, which will come next. However, we have to put first things first before we start talking about purchasing or the care of your vehicle.

Insurance: Your Responsibility to You and Your Fellow Drivers

One of the first things that you need to do before hitting the open road is to purchase the proper amount of insurance. The proper amount would be at the very least the amount to keep you legal, and if needed, take care of you and possibly other drivers if you are at fault in the event that you are in an accident. As a side note, if you plan to finance your car, financial institutions require you to have full coverage insurance. They want to know that they will still be paid back if your car is "totaled" in a flood or hail storm, for example.

Now I know that as you read this you may be saying to yourself, "Well, this is pretty fundamental..." However, the number of uninsured motorists nationwide is alarming. How often have you heard stories of a friend or a loved one being involved in an accident, just to find out that the other driver had no insurance? Now perhaps the particular type of accident, or what happened to cause the accident, may vary, but one common thread may be that the other driver didn't have any insurance.

Not only is driving without insurance illegal, but it is also very irresponsible. Depending on which research firm you talk to, the rate of uninsured motorists is as high as 16%. According to The Center for Insurance Policy and Research, that number is a more conservative 13%, or roughly about one in eight drivers being without the adequate amount of auto insurance.

What does this mean to you? Well first off, this means we must purchase uninsured motorists (UM) insurance in one form or another. Why do we all need this type of insurance? After all, is it that necessary? The answer is a resounding yes. If you are unfortunate enough to be involved in a car accident with an uninsured or underinsured motorist, who's going to pay for damages and possible medical expenses in the event that they are at fault? It's the UM insurance that pays for the medical bills, lost wages and pain and suffering. UM insurance is also important if you get struck by a hit and run driver.

Do yourself a favor and purchase insurance. One of the top reasons motorists give for not having adequate insurance is that it's too expensive and that they couldn't afford it. However, the truth is you can't afford not to have insurance. Can you afford losing work time to show up for court hearings? Or, can you afford to lose your driving privileges? Most of us can't. I would recommend that you shop around, as insurance rates vary widely from company to company. Most offer discounts for this or for that. In most cases the longer you stay with one company, and stay accident free, the better your rates will be. It normally doesn't save you money, in the long run, by jumping from one insurance company to another on a constant basis just because they send you some junk mail promising that they can save you a few bucks. I get those all of the time, but every time I put them to the test, they can't give me any lower insurance rates than the company that I've been with for thirty years. In most cases, they can't even come close. I will add, one common thread between all insurance companies is that the more tickets you get (i.e., if you drive recklessly) the higher your insurance rates will go. So shop around and ask some family members or friends which companies they use, then do some comparisons.

Set up Roadside Assistance in Your Phone's Directory

One of the things that I like to recommend to customers of mine is that if they plan to travel any distances from their homes, they may want to purchase a roadside assistance plan. There are many companies with different plans available. AAA comes to mind and is the most popular, but they are just one of them. Cell phone companies and auto insurance companies now offer roadside assistance for a minimal monthly or annual fee.

If you plan to purchase a new car, many vehicle manufactures offer an initial roadside assistance program, so ask your salesperson about it. However, don't get the roadside assistance program confused with an aftermarket warranty offered for some used cars; they are different and we'll talk about those later on in Chapter 2. General Motors (Chevrolet, Buick, Cadillac and GMC) offers a free initial On Star subscription. After the initial subscription runs out you have the opportunity to purchase the renewal.

Back to AAA: AAA has three levels of membership, depending on how much or how far you travel and the age of your vehicle. Each membership has a certain number of tows and distance per year, so you'll have to decide which plan is right for you. For example, AAA's Classic Membership allows up to four tows per year and they will cover up to five miles each; after that, the meter starts running and you flip the bill for any additional mileage. This wouldn't be much good if you travel a lot and go extended distances. However, if you stay close to your hometown and rarely travel, this may be right for you. Most people get the Plus Membership. With this you get up to four tows per year but they'll cover your mileage up to 100 miles. The Premium Membership is about the same, except one of your tows can be up to 200 miles. There are also other benefits to your membership, so for more information go to www.aaa.com. Okay, you're probably wondering how much AAA is paying me to pitch their service. They aren't paying me a single penny. I make these recommendations after years of working with customers and, shall we say, their roadside situations. Again, shop around for the best deal. The auto insurance company that you already use or the cell phone service that you already have may have the service available. However they may not have the mileage allowance that AAA has, nor the other benefits.

The nice thing about purchasing a roadside assistance plan is that, if your car happens to break down, you don't have to look for a towing service. The particular roadside assistance company that you are with will dispatch the towing service. If you have a reputable towing service in your vicinity that you would like to deal with for local towing, then store their phone number in your cell phone so that you will always have it with you. Also, for those long trips, add your roadside assistance number to your phone along with all of your other important phone numbers. Most roadside assistance companies have nationwide service. This means that no matter where you're at, you have the peace of mind knowing that help is just a phone call away.

Don't Become a Statistic

Most of us, at some point in our lives, get the feeling that we're ten feet tall and bullet-proof. We may try to perform daring stunts on our bicycles when we are young. I remember walking home from the candy store one winter day many years ago. My cousin and I didn't want to add the fifteen extra minutes it would have taken us if we walked home via the road, so we decided to take a short cut across a somewhat frozen lake. We knew full well that the lake wasn't safe as we could see water filling in the footprints that we left behind.

As we get older and more seasoned in our decision-making process, we try to weigh the risks we take a little more heavily. Therefore, we should weigh those risks more as we start driving. The more you drive the more you see situations along the roadways that make you take notice. Perhaps a patrol car has a vehicle pulled over to the side of the road, or maybe an ambulance or fire truck is on the scene of an accident. The point is, all of these things that we observe happening around us should in fact help us to become better drivers, more aware. By being more aware of our surroundings, we are able to be more in control and not another statistic along the side of the road.

That Text Can Wait!

Have you ever just sat somewhere and watched people as they drive by? I don't mean stare at them in a creepy sort of way, but just watch them? If not, you're in for a treat. When you have a few moments of spare time, try to find a busy intersection somewhere or maybe get a cup of coffee or hot chocolate at a coffee shop, and just sit and watch the commuters. Pay close attention to what they're doing. You will be alarmed to see how many drivers are either texting or talking on their phones. Some are even surfing the web while trying to guide a 6000-pound missile down the road.

Many accidents occur when a driver's attention is not focused on their driving. According to www.textinganddrivingsafety.com, approximately one out of four car crashes involved cell phones. How many fatalities does it take to get people to stop texting while they drive? Many states have laws against texting and driving, making it a moving violation. Remember your insurance rates? Get a ticket and rates go up! Texting can wait: if your attention is distracted for just a few seconds, everybody loses; it's just not worth it.

If you are a busy professional who spends a lot of time in the car, sometimes your car is your office. Many vehicles are becoming available that allow hands-free communication. It's preferred that the driver not be distracted by phone calls at all, but if you must, use a voice activated hands-free device.

The Need for Speed

Do you ever find yourself having the need for speed? Admittedly, when I was younger I did and as a result I paid a few tickets for my foolishness. Boy, was I young and naïve. Remember those insurances rates we discussed earlier? Yup, I paid the price in more than just the speeding ticket.

The majority of drivers find themselves, at one time or another, in a situation where they can justify or come up with a "good excuse" for speeding. Or, at least they thought it was a good excuse right up to the point where the police officer handed them a speeding citation.

Speeding is a very serious offense and shouldn't be taken lightly. According to the national average, approximately one-third of all traffic fatalities are speed related. There are two categories of speed related offenses or crashes. The first is pretty self-explanatory: exceeding the posted speed limit (EPSL). The second, driving too fast for conditions (DTFFC), is not so cut and dried.

EPSL: Exceeding the Posted Speed Limit

You may think that going a few miles over the posted speed limit doesn't seem to be a big deal, reasoning that everybody does it, right? Yes, many people speed on a regular basis, but is that a good enough reason to make yourself susceptible to receiving speeding citations and probable insurance rate hike? Yes, if you make it a habit of speeding, then at some point or another it'll catch up with you. Not only that, the way you drive affects others directly. For example, if you are a new driver you may not have experienced this yet, but you will. You will see the occasional reckless driver who is for one reason or another going at high speed swerving in and out of traffic, and this will affect your driving. Your first reaction is to get angry with them. "What are they, nuts?" You may think this to yourself or yell it out to your passengers. This is the time to stay cool and not react aggressively, as some do.

The best way to react to reckless drivers is to drive defensively. I'm not making excuses for the other driver, but at that very moment, you don't know what's going through their head. Are they angry about something or at someone? Are they trying to get a loved one to the hospital? On the other hand, maybe they're just listening to some upbeat music and in their own little world and not paying attention. The point is that the best way to keep you and your loved ones out of harm's way is to always drive defensively. It's not a competition to see who owns the roadways, or a game of May the Biggest Vehicle Win. If you see someone ahead of you driving recklessly, then back off slightly and let them go. If you see someone coming up behind you at a high speed, stay in the right lane, maintaining our current speed; let them go around.

Reckless speeding can be a hazardous lifestyle for you and others. One day it will catch up to you—it always does. Drive defensively at all times. Obey the posted speed limits, leave racing to the professionals or movie stunts, and enjoy your driving experience.

DTFFC: Driving Too Fast for Conditions

Driving too fast for conditions is something that just takes some experience and sometimes a little common sense to overcome. Now you may think that the phrase "driving too fast for conditions" only pertains to driving in adverse weather conditions. However, this is not the case.

Driving too fast for conditions involves driving too fast for traffic volume or condition. In other words, if there is traffic congestion due to construction, commuter traffic or an accident, and you continue at the speed you would be driving in the absence of these factors, this is driving too fast for conditions—slow down. If you're feeling unwell or tired, or perhaps maybe under a lot of stress or upset, you may be driving too fast for conditions. The term "conditions" is a broad term covering anything that could cause a hazard if driving faster than your reaction time, the capability of the vehicle you're driving to handle the situation or incident, or possibly the combination of both. Although you may be driving within the posted speed limits, you may still receive a citation if the officer deems that you were driving too fast for conditions.

In northern climates, snow and ice is a condition that northerners learn to deal with. A safe driver will always analyze the condition and capabilities of their vehicle, be aware of the traffic around them and drive accordingly. Notice that I put both the condition and capabilities of your vehicle and awareness of surrounding traffic in the same sentence. These go hand and hand, period!

During the winter months with snow covered road conditions, if you're driving a four-wheel drive vehicle, in great shape and with good tires, you may actually be able to safely travel faster than the little old man driving the 1997 Ford Taurus, with tires on it that should have been replaced two seasons ago. Should he be on the road in these conditions? Maybe not. However, the fact is that he is on the road and you, as a safe driver, will take that into consideration by not flying by him, swerving in and out of traffic. That would be a traffic accident just waiting to happen, which could have been avoided.

In the southern states, except on rare occasions, drivers usually don't have to contend with snow or ice. Nonetheless, heavy rains or fog can hand out some equally challenging driving conditions. It's not worth injuring or possibly killing yourself or someone else on the roadways to shave ten minutes off your travel time. Unfortunately, there are far too many multiple car accidents caused by driving too fast in dense fog. The problem arises when motorists cannot see far enough ahead of them to come to a complete stop in time, out of harm's way. Again, all of these examples are to encourage you to slow down a bit if conditions, whatever they are, don't permit you to travel at the posted speed limit.

The point of this section of the book is not to scare the novice or new driver. However, a certain amount of fear may be healthy, and may keep you alive. The purpose is to educate: the more you know, the more prepared you'll be in the event that you run into these conditions. If the weather forecast is for severe weather, perhaps delay your trip. If you're tired, safely pull over and get some rest. If the medication you just took makes you drowsy, get someone else to drive you or postpone your trip. These are things to consider before getting behind the wheel.

"I'm Okay; I've Only Had a Couple of Drinks"

Back when I was younger—I was nineteen, if my memory serves me right—I was stationed in San Diego while doing my stint in the United States Navy. I was out for some training that the Navy had given me orders to attend. As class neared its end it was customary at the time for someone to throw a graduation party. In the case of our class, it was the oldest of us all. He was a bow-legged, bull-riding fellow. I forget his name, so for the purpose of this story we'll just call him Mike. Mike sure knew how to throw a party. It was at that party that I did something very stupid and something that I will never forget.

Being young and with some of my class buddies, we drank some beer—a lot of beer. The consumption of the beer wasn't the thing that was so bad, although maybe the excess that we consumed wasn't the brightest thing to do. As the party started to wind down the guys were starting to leave and go back to their barracks or apartments. When I got ready to leave, Mike asked me if I was okay to drive. I replied, "Yeah, I'm okay." He asked, "Are you sure?" Again, I replied, "I'm okay; I've only had a couple of drinks." He knew better than that, but he let me go anyway. Little did I know that while driving back to my apartment I would black out. I did make it home all right, but to this day, I have no idea how I got there. Thankfully no one got hurt, or worse—killed. The next day I was terrified. I had no knowledge of the last portion of my trip home the night before. That was an incredibly irresponsible and dangerous thing for me to do. I've never repeated that since.

According to the CDC (Center for Disease Control), in 2013 nearly one-third of all traffic fatalities were the result of alcohol impaired driving. In 2012, over 1.3 million drivers were arrested while driving under the influence of drugs or alcohol. Over the years, state and local police agencies have taken a much tougher stance on driving under the influence.

What used to be a slap on the wrist and a night in the local jail is now some serious time and stiff fines. When you add it all up, according to some experts, a non-jury no damage DUI (<u>D</u>riving while <u>U</u>nder the <u>I</u>nfluence) case can cost between $5,000 to $10,000, or even more. This includes court costs, attorney fees, substance abuse counseling, license reinstatement, ignition interlock system (if ordered by the judge), increased insurance rates and loss of income from sitting in jail. If there is damage to someone's vehicle or personal property, the costs start to add up even higher. For what it costs in pain and suffering for either you or someone else, it's simply not worth the short lived thrill of being intoxicated and then getting behind the wheel. Either have a sober designated driver or don't drink if you have to drive.

Topics with Purpose

I purposely chose to talk about these three topics because as a driver, these are the three top traffic fatality concerns: texting while driving, speeding, and driving while under the influence of alcohol or drugs. Driving can be a very enjoyable yet serious privilege. If there is any one thing that I would like for you to take away from this book it is the importance of safe driving. I want each and every one of you to stay alive and safe for your children, grandchildren and even your great grandchildren, or other loved ones' sakes. A simple lapse in judgment can have lifelong repercussions. Reaching for that phone to read a text, speeding to make it through that next stop light before it turns red, or deciding to get behind the wheel when you should have handed your keys over to someone else can irreversibly change your or someone else's life forever.

Keep Your Hands on the Wheel, Getting Pulled Over

I think the most horrifying feeling that I've had while driving is the feeling you get, in the pit of your stomach, when you see that police car in your rear-view mirror, and they flip their lights on, signaling for you to find a safe place and then pull over. I'm not proud to say that in my earlier years I was the recipient of a few tickets—and not the lottery kind either, the traffic citation kind. How foolish I felt after considering that each one was completely avoidable. However, I accepted responsibility, paid my fine and tried to learn something from the experience.

While on the subject of being pulled over, do you know where your driver's registration and proof of insurance is at this very moment? If they are in a special envelope or folder in your vehicle's glove box, good for you, you get an A+. If you're not sure where they are, or you left them in the stack of mail on your dresser or desk, go get them now. Find an envelope or small folder and mark on it "Registration and Insurance," and now put those two documents inside of either the envelope or folder. Now you should put this very important documentation inside of your vehicle, preferably in a place that's easy to get to, like the glove box. The reason for this is that if you are asked for your paperwork by a police officer, you shouldn't have to shuffle around or pull out a pouch that may be large enough to hold a handgun.

Although getting pulled over by the police may be a stressful event, here are some tips to help you through it. Above all, don't argue or show an attitude with the officer. You may think that you know your rights, but unless you're an attorney it's best to keep your opinions to yourself. If they were intending to let you off with a warning, they certainly won't if you're showing attitude.

- Don't panic: You may feel angry, nervous or confused but rest assured, almost everyone, at some point in their life, will go through the very same thing.

- Pull over to the right side of the road: Use your turn signal and pull over as soon as you can safely do so. The officer will understand if you have to drive a short distance to safely pull off to the side of the road. Simply turn on your flashers to acknowledge to the officer that you are intending to pull off. It's safer for you and the officer if you are not in an area where traffic is heavy and where either one of you could be hurt. Do not pull off on the left side of the road.
- Turn off the ignition and place the keys on the dash.
- Turn on your interior light: If it is between dusk and dawn, turn on your interior lights. This is for your and the officer's safety. In some states it's the law.
- Keep your hands on the wheel: Keep your hands in plain sight so that the officer can see them; preferably keep them on the steering wheel.
- Comply with the officer's request: The officer will ask you for your license, registration and proof of insurance. If you have to reach for your paperwork let the officer know beforehand exactly what you are doing. If you are legally carrying a weapon, convey that, and the weapon's location, to the officer as well. If you have a concealed and carry permit or you have hunting equipment in the back, let the officer know. On the subject of weapons, when you are traveling through different states or municipalities, do your homework before traveling to make sure it is legal for you to transport those weapons.
- Stay in your vehicle: Once the officer collects your documents, he will go back to his police cruiser. Do not get out of your vehicle unless he asks you to do so.
- Ask the officer to clarify if needed: Depending on the reason you were pulled over, you may receive a traffic citation or a ticket. If you are unclear as to the charges, ask him to clarify them.
- Merge safely back into the traffic: When the officer is finished, carefully merge back into traffic.

Don't assume that the officer knows that you are a perfect, law-abiding citizen. Their job can be very dangerous. Therefore, when you are in your vehicle, don't make any sudden moves. Communicate to the officer what you are intending to do before you do it. At night, officers generally don't mind if you slowly proceed to a well-lit area. If it is dark, officers will use flashlights and spotlights to help illuminate the area; again, it's for your safety.

Chapter 2: So You Want to Buy a Car

Now that you've gotten some driving experience under your belt, you're ready to take the plunge and purchase your first set of wheels. What is the purpose of the vehicle that you would like to purchase? Do you want to get something that will allow you to commute back and forth to work with the occasional short trip? What about the ride: are you looking for luxury or something a little more sporty? Do you live in town or out in the country? What are the roads like? Are they smooth or rough? How about the weather, are you in a northern climate where you may get a lot of snow where you will be driving?

One aspect that I recommend to my customers to consider is the long-term cost of owning the vehicle that they are about to purchase. It's not just the initial sale; it's the insurance costs, the fuel economy. That's a big one with the fuel prices fluctuating more than the stock market. How much will the maintenance or upkeep be? These are all important things to take into consideration when preparing for your car purchase.

When buying a used vehicle, especially an older one with higher miles, maintenance and repair bills are a part of life. The first thing I urge prospective buyers to do is to save up a minimum of $500, but preferably $1,500, for an emergency fund for vehicle repairs. This will make the news that you will occasionally hear from your technician more tolerable. If he says that you need $800 in repairs and you have nothing saved up, that's when the panic sets in and possibly that much needed repair is put off. If money is in your auto repair account then the estimate that he or she gives you will be much easier to digest.

As I sit here writing this book, I have a customer who needs $600 in brake repairs. They don't have the money to get the repairs done and they are very upset, as they have no transportation. Another customer has an 07 Chevy Impala that has worn-out brakes and the ball joints are loose and ready to come apart, total cost $1,800. Looking in the back seat, I see a child's car seat. If you're not doing it for you, do it for your precious cargo. So get that money saved up in your auto emergency repair fund. Do whatever it takes, and keep it there. It's not for a shopping spree or that once in a lifetime concert. It's for those repairs that WILL arise, it's just a matter of when. Okay, let's talk cars!

Buy with Purpose

Let's first start by determining the main purpose of the vehicle that you want to purchase. This will be something that you may want to ponder a bit. Now, I can make several recommendations to you, but they would be based on what I enjoy driving, my preferences or on my economics. For example, I come from a General Motors family; nearly all of us drive GM. I enjoy driving and working on them. However, if your dad works for Ford or Uncle Ed is a diehard Chrysler or Dodge man, then you will get different recommendations from them. For that reason, I will recommend classes or sizes of vehicles. From there you can go to the specific manufacturers' websites and make comparisons. There are independent websites that will allow you to make comparisons of vehicles across different manufacturers.

The purpose and size of the vehicle you would like to purchase will go hand and hand. It doesn't make a lot of sense to buy a two-seat mini-compact car if you will be adding to your family soon, unless of course it is a second vehicle with the primary purpose of urban commuting to work. Likewise, if you're on a limited income, and you live alone, driving back and forth to work in a Ford Expedition or Chevy Suburban, by yourself, will add up to more money in the fuel tank and less in your pocket. As with many things, there are exceptions to the rules. If your job requires you to haul inventory or tools, then you may need a little extra room.

For reference, a table that lists the vehicle classes and how they translate into size, this and much more information can be found on www.fueleconomy.gov. You can make comparisons from one vehicle to another for up to four vehicles. Although the web site is geared mostly toward Hybrid and Plug-In technologies, it does provide some good resources to help the car buyer do their homework before shopping. Fuel efficiency information is readily available on the mentioned website, and this may be one of the determining factors for making your final decision.

Size Matters

The technical details I will leave for the search engines and websites. Instead, I will break it down in layman's terms for you, keeping it simple. Obviously when I list the occupants, it's going to depend on their size. However, in most cases, when adults are listed, we are talking about an average height of approximately 5"6' with a medium build.

Broken down into the simplest of terms, passenger cars fit into three categories. An economy or compact car can usually "comfortably" fit two adults and two children. Midsize or intermediate can generally fit four adults, and full-size vehicles will usually accommodate five adults.

SUVs typically come in three sizes: compact, which seats four adults; standard size, which usually accommodates five; and the full-size SUV that can carry about seven passengers. Sometimes you may hear someone mention "crossover," also called a crossover utility vehicle or CUV. In simplest terms, the best way to describe a crossover is a combination of an SUV and a station wagon. Usually it has the four-wheel or all-wheel drive of the SUV and the comfort and ride of a station wagon.

There are also three van classes. Mini-vans seat from six to eight people. The full-sized van can seat ten to fifteen passengers, depending on whether it is an extended version or not. The other class of van is the cargo van; this usually seats two adults with a whole lot of room for tools or cargo in the back. Usually, cargo vans won't have any windows in the back.

Lastly, there are pickup trucks. Again, for simplicity's sake there are three classes of pickup trucks that the average consumer will be concerned with. The first two classes are the small to midsize (quarter ton) and full size (half ton). Then there are the heavy-duty trucks (three-quarter and one ton). All of these trucks can be purchased with a standard cab (which seats two), or extended cab (which usually seats two adults and two children). The crew cab, which previously was reserved for full-sized trucks and above but can now be found in the midsized trucks, can seat four or five.

As you can see, even though I broke down the categories the way I did, it can still be a little confusing. We didn't even touch on the size of the hybrid or electric vehicles. I'm getting a little ahead of myself, but these two websites, www.nadaguides.com and www.kbb.com, have many excellent tools for finding technical data on new and used vehicles. You may have to dig a bit but most of the information is there. For what you can't find while researching here, try the manufacturers websites. However, while navigating the various websites, be cautious of some of the ads while yet being an informed shopper.

Therefore, if you are single and on a limited income, you may want to buy a smaller more compact car. If you are a family of four, you may be thinking of getting a midsize to full-size car. Or, perhaps crossover or a small SUV would fit your style. If you live in the south where it rarely snows, if at all, you may not find a need for an SUV, unless the terrain is rough or wet. On the other hand, living in the northern climates, where it snows often, a vehicle with four-wheel drive will come in handy. Ultimately, this is a decision that only you can make. I will urge the reader not to buy anything that is bigger than they will need right now or in the near future.

When and Where to Start Looking

Many times I will have a customer come up to me and ask where they should start looking for a new or used car. Even though they may have lived in the area for many years, they wouldn't have a clue where they could get an honest deal or a good vehicle. At times a customer will be in a hurry because their vehicle has just been condemned; or their technician advises that they really should get something a bit more reliable so that they don't get stranded somewhere. The absolute worst time to be looking for another vehicle is when yours is broken down or for some other reason undrivable. This is when a majority of HUGE mistakes are made in purchasing a car. One feels panicked, rushed and perhaps a little overwhelmed at the prospect of acquiring another vehicle so that one can get to work or make that long-awaited trip.

At some time, everything wears out, so plan ahead to buy or replace your car. Having a good relationship with your automotive technician is very beneficial in the long run. Just as you wouldn't jump from doctor to doctor, once you have found a good and trusted tech, stick with them (more about that in Chapter 6). The point that I'm making is that if you maintain a good relationship with your technician, they can keep a close eye on your car for you while they are doing the regular preventative maintenances and oil changes. So when it is time to look for another car or truck, they will have advised you, possibly several months ahead of time, to start looking. This allows you to have a more relaxed or even laid back approach to car buying. This too, gives you a buying advantage, which I'll explain.

When a car buyer is not in a hurry and has financially prepared themselves either by saving or securing a low interest loan through their credit union or bank, they walk into the car dealership with the advantage. By nature, car salesmen are dealers: they like to close the deal. It's their livelihood, it's the reason dealerships exist. You, on the other hand, if you've planned well ahead, don't NEED the deal. If you don't like the terms of the contract or deal, you can and should reject it and counter-offer, or get up and leave. If you aren't pushed, or in a hurry, you are in charge of the deal. You've got all day, week, month or more to find the deal that meets YOUR needs, not somebody else's. This is why it's crucial to plan ahead and not wait until your present vehicle is ready for the scrap yard.

Part of preparing is determining how much you want to spend. Obviously, the more money you have saved, the newer and perhaps better car you'll be able to purchase. You can get some good deals with less money, but you may have to search a little harder for them.

There are a couple of ways to look at used car shopping. You can pay more up front on a newer vehicle and not have to worry so much on repairs for the first few years, or you can pay less up front and expect to put more into the vehicle with repairs. This will depend on your comfort level, and whether or not you can easily deal with tow trucks and missed work or appointments. Ideally, I like to find a vehicle no more than four or five years old and with no more than 50,000 miles on the odometer. The original owner took the hit on the depreciation and I get a vehicle that, if taken care of, can be driven for six to eight years or more.

If money is an issue, then often family members or friends can be a good source for a used vehicle. You know the person who is selling it and you will probably have access to all of the service records or receipts. This will usually be your best deal; family members aren't typically looking to make a big profit selling their cars like dealerships or used car lots. In most cases, they are pleased to get a slightly better price than the trade-in value at a dealership. Dealerships will typically only give them trade-in value, which depending on the make, model and year could be thousands of dollars less than if it was sold to a private individual. So, if Aunt Betty is planning to trade her four-year-old Buick in for a new model, tell her that you'll give her a few hundred over the dealer trade-in value. It's win-win for both of you: she gets more than trade-in value for her car, and you get a sweet deal on a good reliable car.

While on the subject, if you want the ease of trading in your old car at the time you purchase the new one, be advised the convenience will come at a cost—sometimes a big cost. As mentioned in the previous paragraph, dealerships will generally give you the trade-in value. The exception to this rule is if you are trading in a vehicle that is in high demand, such as special edition Mustangs, Corvettes and the like. In these cases the customer may get a little better trade-in allowance. Generally speaking, though, if you have the time and patience, you will come out ahead if you sell your car privately rather than trading it in, with the difference sometimes being in the thousands of dollars.

Put Them to the Test and Then Buy From the Best

Being a frugal car shopper is like anything else: do your homework and know where to go for the best deal. If you are buying new, ask friends or family which dealerships have the best reputation during and after the sale is made. In most cases, this is where you will get your best information from. A bad dealer will have a reputation that gets around like wildfire. You are looking for a long-term relationship, because you will undoubtedly be buying several vehicles in your lifetime and it is always easier going back to a place that has dealt honestly with you in the past. If you have two or three dealerships in town that sell the same makes and models of cars, put them to the test and then buy from the best. In other words, if you haven't yet established that relationship, put the dealerships to the test to see which one wants your business, who will go the extra mile to earn your loyalty.

Imagine a time when you have gone to a store to purchase something, perhaps it's a small appliance of some sort, let's say a toaster. You aren't sure exactly which of two models you want, so you have a few questions to ask a sales associate. You see the sales associates there, but they don't come to ask if they can help you. You may even get one or two of them to look directly at you, just to go off and help another customer who wants to purchase a big ticket item like a side-by-side refrigerator with a built-in ice maker or wine cooler in it. So it is with car dealers: test them to see what their customer relation etiquette is. If you go to three different dealers and one of them has excellent customer relation policies in place, go with them. They may not be the cheapest game in town, but in the long term you will be more content going to a dealership you know will return phone calls, takes the time to answer all of your questions and treats you with respect. To emphasize this aspect, let me relate a story to you.

About twenty-five years ago I knew this man who was in his early sixties. He was a contractor by trade, and his company built houses. He was always busy going from one job site to another helping his guys out. Long days were the norm for him. One day his old truck had hauled its last load of lumber, so he decided to go buy a new truck that very day. He had been contemplating it for a while and he knew just what he wanted. So he had one of his workers drop him off at a new car dealership. Wearing that day's dirty work clothes, worn boots and his hair still messed up, he walked into the dealership looking like a hobo. As he looked at a couple of new trucks he was amazed that none of the sales representatives came over to ask him if they could help, nor did anybody acknowledge him. He asked for help, just to be told that he would be helped in a few minutes. As he waited, he kept looking. He could see available salesmen that weren't helping anybody else. After about a half an hour of waiting for help, he reached into his pockets and pulled out his hands that were filled with one hundred dollar bills, held them up in the air and yelled, "Maybe the next dealership I go to will be more willing to take my money!" as he walked out the door.

Now this isn't the norm. In most cases, sales reps are more than eager to come help and ask you if you are in need of help. The point is this: if a new or used car dealership truly wants your business, they will bend over backwards to help you out, make you feel comfortable, answer all of your questions and treat you with respect. This takes some skill on the part of the sales associate. They should treat you like a human being, not their next meal ticket. They should never hurry you or try to power-sell you into something you don't want.

Buy Here, Pay Here

Over the past few years, with the slowing of the economy, "buy here pay here" used car lots have become more popular. I would strongly recommend staying away from these lots. The vehicles that they have to offer are overpriced and the "in house" credit comes with a much higher interest rate. Credit unions or your personal bank are some good sources to start with. New car deals can be pretty sweet, especially when the dealers are trying to move out the prior year's inventory. If you have good credit, sometimes the financing department at your dealership can help find you a good or even zero interest rate. But before signing on the line, check with your personal financial institution first.

Buy here, pay here establishments are, with few exceptions, acting as both used car dealer and in house lending institution. Many times you may see ads listing a very low weekly payment, but in the long run you will end up paying much more than what the vehicle is actually worth. Several years ago I had a couple of friends who, through some bad decision making, had developed poor credit ratings. They purchased cars at a local "buy here, pay here" used car lot, and they were very sorry they did. One of them purchased a car that died a slow death, but he still had several months before it was paid off. The other missed his weekly payment and his car was quickly and without notice repossessed.

The buy here, pay here dealers prey on those with poor credit. Most conventional banks or credit unions want some sort of credit worthiness before lending. If you have a poor credit rating, and the normal source for lending is not available, buy here, pay here lots are there to scoop the unsuspecting buyer up.

Because they don't have the lending power that banks or credit unions have, buy here, pay here lots are gambling that the buyer won't just drive off with the car never to be seen again. Therefore, they will want a large down payment of some sort to act as security against loss. According to www.lemonusedcarlaw.com the interest rates can be in the double digits. It's not uncommon to see interest rates as high as 25% or 30% and vehicles selling for double or more their actual value.

Unfortunately, many young drivers get caught up in situations where they feel that this is the only place that they can go to get a vehicle, but I would recommend these establishments only as a last resort. In addition, by all means, have the car that you intend to buy inspected by your technician or at least a third party. Also, make sure that you make your weekly or monthly payment not just on time but early if possible. This goes for any car loan. Don't risk getting your car repossessed and your credit ruined. It's not unusual for the same repossessed vehicle to be sold several times by the same car lot due to missed car payments. They keep your down payment and any payments you've made, and they get to put it back out on the lot to sell again.

New vs. Used: The Pros and Cons

When you start looking, don't just settle or buy on a whim, get a vehicle that you feel comfortable purchasing. Too many times I have seen a slick salesperson talk someone into a vehicle that they really didn't intend to buy. In other words, they walk into a new or used car dealership looking for one thing and leaving with something that they weren't planning to buy. Remember, you have to live with your decision until you decide to sell it or trade it in for a different vehicle. For some salespeople, once you're gone, they just move on to the next potential customer. The majority of them work partially if not totally off commission. Therefore, you know whose interest they are looking after.

Once you've decided on the vehicle that best fits you, take advantage of any incentives that the dealership may be offering. This is especially true when you are buying new. When a new model year comes out, usually in the fall or early winter months, dealerships want to move out the prior year's models and inventory to make room for the new. January is often a great month to buy. This is good news for those looking to buy new but who don't need to have the absolute newest model. So if you aren't in a hurry, new model year roll out is a great time to buy and many times the buyer can save hundreds or even thousands. Along that same line, manufacturers offer rebates and incentives for buying. Sometimes they will take a predetermined amount off the price. Other times, the dealership or manufacturer will offer credit at ridiculously low interest rates (if you have good credit).

An advantage of buying new is that the vehicle you are looking at will have the latest technology in it. This is particularly good when it comes to its safety rating. Newer cars will come standard with the updated supplemental restraint systems (air bags) installed. Traction control and antilock brake systems are a benefit that make driving in adverse weather conditions much safer. Anti-theft systems come standard on most vehicles now, making installation by an aftermarket company all but obsolete. Last but not least, generally on the newer vehicle you will get better fuel economy, and as mentioned earlier, fuel economy can be a determining factor on what you end up buying. Today's vehicles are designed to squeeze every possible mile out of a gallon of gas.

Buying a, shall we say, gently used vehicle can have its own advantages. The biggest advantage, and the one I like the most is the savings. As I mentioned earlier, by purchasing a gently used vehicle, you get all of the benefits of a new car but without the cost. The previous owner bought it new or perhaps it was a demonstration model that was recently turned in. In any event, the frugal buyer can save thousands by purchasing a model that is only one or two years old with less than 20,000 miles on it and still under the manufacturer's warranty. Most of these are considered "certified pre-owned" vehicles as opposed to "used."

Avoid the Rental Return

I would advise the reader to avoid buying a "rental return." These vehicles have been run hard and in most cases not maintained the way they should be. Rental companies are in business for one thing, to RENT vehicles, not sell them. So if a vehicle isn't being driven by a renter then the rental company is not making money. For this reason, they try to keep the vehicles on the road with a wide variety of drivers behind the wheel. The businesswoman in town for a meeting, a factory employee in town helping to get machinery online or a college graduate that just flew in for a job interview. All of these drivers have different driving habits, and some, knowing that it's not their car, don't treat it as such.

Another point that I would like to make is that, while rental companies may try to provide the minimum required maintenance to their vehicles, this doesn't mean that they are well taken care of. I've rented vehicles for business trips and found them barely tolerable at times, while other times the vehicle was quite satisfactory. However, if a vehicle is only two years old and you find that the steering wheel is thirty degrees off center and the brakes pulsate violently when you try to stop, it's been driven hard and not maintained properly. If you do decide to purchase a rental return, demand lower than book value and expect to invest some of your own cash on some repairs.

Don't confuse these vehicles with fleet returns, which are an entirely different proposition. Many times a fleet return may have had only one or two different drivers. Many companies will provide fleet vehicles for some of their employees. They may use this vehicle for commuting back and forth to work or the occasional business trip. A fleet returned vehicle could be a good deal; again, as with any used car purchase, caution should be exercised. If the mileage seems excessively high for the year, or it just doesn't feel right while driving, then you may want to pass it up.

If Unsure, Start Here . . .

Remember this website: www.carfax.com. Perhaps you've heard of it. If you have, please humor me while I explain this great tool to those who haven't heard of it yet. Carfax is a website that allows the buyer to do some car shopping and research all in the comfort of their living room or bedroom, while in their slippers. The best way to describe Carfax is that it's like doing a background check on the prospective car that you are considering buying. Many dealerships will now offer to give you a free Carfax report when you're there shopping. A Carfax report can tell you how many owners a car has had. It can also tell you if it has a salvage title, in other words if it has been in a wreck and been repaired. The report often tells you about the service history.

When the unsure shopper is looking for a used vehicle and they don't know where to start, there is a section on www.carfax.com that is called "Find a used car." Just click on the button and follow the prompts, and they will walk you through the search process. When you find a vehicle that you are interested in, click on the "view free Carfax report" button. You will then be able to view a detailed history of the vehicle, including owner history, any accident history and service history. This is a great tool to help weed out the bad apples and save you time, and I've used it quite often.

You may have an acquaintance or friend give you a great lead on a car. Simply get the vehicle identification number, also called the VIN. To get the VIN, go to the driver's door and open it up. Now look at the door pillar where the door closes and latches to it. There should be a sticker with a seventeen-digit number that is alphanumeric; this is your VIN. If it's not seventeen digits then it may be a pre-1981 vehicle. Now go to www.carfax.com and click on the "get Carfax reports" button. Type in the VIN. In most cases, if there are any red flags, they will show up in the report. If you are buying from a private party, and you are doing your own research, then you will have to pay approximately forty dollars for the report. But in the long run, forty bucks is a small price to pay to find out that the car that you almost bought needed several hundred dollars' worth of suspension work due to a prior wreck. As of the printing of this book, fifty dollars gets you five Carfax reports within sixty days. So, if you're not happy with the first vehicle, you can keep shopping without purchasing additional individual reports, a nice feature!

Carfax is not failproof; the information is only as good as the data that was acquired. However, it is much better than going in blind, with no information. I've come to trust them over the years.

Certified Pre-Owned or Used?

Therefore, you're probably asking, "What's the difference between a 'certified pre-owned' (or CPO) car and a used car?" You've probably heard the term thrown around on the radio or in TV spot ads. Here are the two main differences: a used car is just that, a used car with all of its parts, some of which may need to be replaced. You usually buy it in an "as is" condition. It may come with tires that will need to be replaced soon or a radio that doesn't work. Sometimes you can negotiate the price down and take it "as is" or pay more for the vehicle and have the seller repair the broken or worn-out items. A certified pre-owned car is one that goes through a rigorous inspection, and if necessary is repaired by factory trained technicians before it ever goes out on the car lot. These vehicles are usually newer and have fewer miles on them than your average used car. Certified pre-owned can take some of the stress or worry out of buying a vehicle. Be aware, however, that some used car lots or "buy here, pay here" lots may advertise that their cars are certified pre-owned, but by whom? I would advise the car shopper to purchase a certified pre-owned vehicle only from a reputable new car dealership.

Domestic, Asian and European: What's the Difference?

In a global economy it is possible to purchase a good reliable vehicle that has parts manufactured all over the world and the vehicle itself assembled in one or more countries. How does this affect you as the consumer? Primarily, it means that you have a plethora of buying options at your disposal. So with names like BMW, Honda, Ford, Chevrolet and the list goes on and on, how do you decide what's best for you? Are you going to be replacing your vehicle every four years or so? If so, then your options may be a little more open. If you can only afford to buy used and will be keeping it until it wears out, then I would steer you into a different direction, and here's why.

When you buy used or pre-owned, which I do quite often, it will require trips to the shop for repairs and replacement of worn items such as brakes, spark plugs, belts and the like. Based on my experience and that of others, vehicles built in Europe tend to be a bit more expensive to maintain and repair. Now before I offend anybody, I need to clarify that these vehicles are amazing vehicles to drive! They offer some of the leading-edge technology, safety equipment and luxury. If you are buying new and money isn't a problem, these are great cars. However, be advised, if you are buying used or pre-owned and you are on a limited income, use great caution when purchasing one of these makes.

Because many of them require more specialized tools and equipment, most independent repair shops limit what repairs they will do to them, which leaves you with just one option: going to the dealership for service. Here is a list of the more common vehicles that are European makes:

- Audi
- BMW
- Land Rover
- Jaguar
- Mini
- Porsche
- Mercedes-Benz
- Volvo
- Saab
- Volkswagen

If you need repairs, and at some point you WILL need repairs, in most cases you will need to go back to the dealership or a shop that specializes in European makes and models. Because these are higher end vehicles, you can expect to pay higher end prices on parts and labor. I've seen many a customer purchase and older BMW or Jaguar thinking, "Oh wow, boy I'm driving in style now!" just to find out that they can't afford the maintenance and repairs on the vehicle.

Another thing to consider when looking at these vehicles is the convenience factor. What I mean is that if you pick up your Audi or Land Rover at the local used car dealership around the corner, this doesn't mean you'll be going back to them for repairs. When the closest dealership or specialty shop is sixty miles away, guess how far you'll be driving to have that water pump replaced or oil leak repaired?

Domestic and Asian Makes

For the most part, for those of you who are buying their first used car, I recommend buying a domestic like General Motors, Ford and Chrysler or an Asian model like a Toyota, Honda or perhaps a Nissan or Subaru. Obviously, with the domestic models, most auto repair facilities are able to work on them. The Asian models I listed are close behind them. Hyundai also makes a good vehicle that many shops can work on. When it comes to finding parts, again they are more readily available and generally less expensive, making your trip to the repair shop less painful than with a European model.

Get a Pre-purchase Inspection, NOT Post Purchase!

Whoever you are purchasing the used car from, ask if you can take the vehicle to your technician for a pre-purchase inspection. If the seller says no, leave the premises, as they may be hiding something. Please don't buy a used car without first getting a pre-purchase inspection from your trusted technician.

Your tech is looking out for YOUR best interests. In most cases, unless you have a trusted sales rep that you happen to know, the seller is looking after THEIR best interests, the money THEY will be making from the sale or the commission. Sometimes the seller will want to go with you to your technicians' shop for the pre-purchase inspection. That's okay, but beforehand inform your tech that you would like to talk to them in private, after the inspection but before the purchase. It can be rather awkward for your tech to tell you that the car you are about to buy is nothing but a glorified boat anchor that's ready for the scrap yard with the seller or salesman standing there.

Getting a second opinion from a trusted source, like your technician, can save you from potentially making a huge mistake that could cost you hundreds, if not thousands of dollars. Many times we get so caught up in the moment, the excitement of buying a car, that we can easily overlook some of the obvious. It can happen to all of us at one time or another.

One time, I was considering buying an older Chevy Camaro. It looked beautiful. It was candy apple red, nice sounding exhaust system and a smooth-running engine. As I was admiring it, looking it over from top to bottom, front to back, the seller told me that it was rock solid. I was impressed; I knew that I just had to have it! However, as I went back to the left rear quarter panel, I noticed a tiny blemish that just didn't look right. While the guy was standing there, I put my finger on the blemish to point it out to him. Instead, my finger went right through the panel. Upon further inspection, other spots on the car were paper thin and just painted over. No proper bodywork had been done, no corrosion removed, just sanded down and painted over. The car was anything but rock solid, and no money exchanged hands on that day!

A friend was looking at a Mercury Capri several years ago and I was asked to go with her and give the car a quick going over, so I did. It didn't look like a bad car for the money, and what the seller was asking appeared to be a fair price. All of the vehicle's fluids were at the proper level and clean. It seemed to run okay, but not great, with the occasional misfire in the engine. I pulled one of the spark plugs out and noticed that the plug was brand new. So I removed another plug. It too was new. I asked the seller how long ago the plugs had been replaced. They said recently, because the car was supposedly due for a tune-up and the plugs were worn out. A red flag went up in my head! (When buying a used vehicle, I like to look at the spark plugs because they can tell you a lot about the condition of the engine.) Something just didn't feel right, so I advised my friend to pass this one up. Unfortunately, she let her excitement get the best of her and she later bought it anyway. About two weeks after she bought the vehicle, that occasional misfire turned into a steady misfire, and the engine then overheated and died. Long story short, I pulled the plugs again and found two of them fouled with antifreeze. The vehicle had a blown head gasket, that the seller did everything they could to cover up.

The moral of these two stories is this: with a trained eye, and a little bit of patience, many times when a seller is trying to cover something up your trained technician can uncover the truth about the condition of the vehicle. They can tell if a vehicle has been run hard or been babied all of its life.

Sometimes the seller may not be fully aware of the condition of the vehicle that they are selling. If your technician finds items that need to be addressed, this can be used to negotiate a lower price if repairs are needed, such as new tires, brakes, etc. Normal wear and tear or perhaps a needed repair is normal when looking at used vehicles. Your technician is there to advise you on such matters. Where his insight is particularly useful is when a dishonest seller is trying to cover something up to try either to get more than the vehicle is worth or to dump the vehicle on some other unsuspecting buyer who comes along. I've been around this business for many years and although most sellers are honest, unfortunately there are those that will sell someone a known defective vehicle and not lose a bit of sleep over it.

So please take away from this section - the importance of making sure you get the inspection BEFORE you purchase the vehicle. Many times we see customers come in for a post purchase inspection, after they have already bought the vehicle, just to find out that they are going to have a very large repair bill. ALWAYS get the inspection before you purchase the vehicle; this is why it is called a "pre-purchase inspection." If you wait, then it's too late, and the results can at times be very discouraging.

The Test Drive: What to Look and Listen For

One of the best diagnostic tools you can have in your arsenal is the "test drive." You can perform this yourself before your technician even gets under the hood or behind the wheel. This simple test can help determine if the vehicle that you are considering buying has suspension, steering, brake, engine, transmission or even electrical issues. This does not necessarily mean that it's not a good value, as long as you know, going into the deal, that you will be putting some money into the vehicle. If possible, try to schedule your test drive on a clear day. You need the roads to be clear of snow or ice, and preferably, not a windy day, as gusts of wind can give an erroneous indication of how a vehicle is handling. Here are a few basic things to look for when you go for a test drive.

- Before you go on a test drive, if you feel comfortable doing so, check the fluid levels and condition. All of the fluids should be translucent and not smell burnt or foul. You shouldn't see any solid particles or shiny debris resembling fine glitter in it.
- As you get into the driver's seat, depress the brake pedal. How does it feel? It should not go to the floor or feel spongy, it should feel firm. When the vehicle is started, it is normal for the brake pedal to feel softer; this is the power brake system doing its job. The brake pedal will also go down a little with the weight of your foot but should never go all of the way to the floor under normal braking.
- While the vehicle's engine is running, there shouldn't be any warning lights illuminated on the dash or driver information center. The engine should run smoothly, no vibrations.
- Okay, now put the vehicle in gear, you shouldn't hear or feel any bangs or clunks; it should be a smooth transition.
- When you start moving, the vehicle and its systems should operate smoothly and without excessive effort. The engine shouldn't sound like it is laboring to get the vehicle moving. The steering and braking should remain smooth and effortless.
- While driving, the steering wheel should not shake or shimmy in your hands. While moving straight, the steering wheel should be centered and the vehicle should not pull to one side or the other. However, don't confuse a "pull" with the normal drift caused by road crown. A pull is just that: you can feel the vehicle pull somewhat aggressively and consistently to the right or to the left. Road crown drift is caused by driving on a road that is higher on one side than the other. Some vehicles will naturally "drift" to the side of the road that's lower.
- During acceleration, the transmission should shift through the gears smoothly with no slipping or banging. To quickly check for this, remember the following: on the traditional

mechanical automatic transmission, you may hear the engine change rotations per minute (RPM) as the vehicle goes through its gear shifting process. If the vehicle has a tachometer, watch the RPM needle when the transmission is shifting. As you are accelerating, the RPM of the engine should drop down each time the transmission up shifts to the next gear. If you hear the engine rev up and the RPMs jump up momentarily before going into the next gear, this indicates an issue with the shifting process. It could be caused by a few different things and if you are still considering purchasing the vehicle, bring it up with your technician so that they can advise you effectively.
- Some vehicles now come with a continuously variable transmission (CVT). You will not feel or hear these shifts into separate gears, as the transitioning process is gradual and smooth. You won't see the tachometer move in the same manner as with the traditional automatic transmission. When working properly, all you will feel is the vehicle accelerating and decelerating very smoothly.
- When braking, again it should be smooth and quiet with no pulsation in the brake pedal or shaking in the steering wheel. Try to find a road that has a few small bumps to test drive on. When going over the bumps, the suspension should be quiet; you shouldn't hear any rattles, squeaks, clunking or banging. Again, if you hear any of these noises, it doesn't necessarily mean the vehicle is not a good deal. After your tech checks is out, it may be a good bargaining chip.

This is not an exhaustive list of things to look for while on a test drive or inspecting a used or certified pre-owned vehicle, but it will help you weed out the bad ones before you pay for a pre-purchase inspection from your technician. If everything feels good on the test drive, arrange for your tech to go over it. This is some cheap insurance and it is worth the money that you pay for the inspection. In addition, don't forget to check the air conditioner, heater, power windows, etc. for proper functionality. Finally, trust your gut. If something just doesn't feel right, it probably isn't. If it walks like a duck and quacks like a duck, it probably isn't a Road Runner (pun intended).

Thinking About Leasing a Car?

Okay, over the years, there has been a lot of going back and forth about the benefits or drawbacks of leasing or buying a vehicle. To some, leasing may be just the ticket to get them into a new car or truck. Here are a few pros and cons about vehicle leases.

The pros are that you'll be in a new vehicle every couple of years or so and the monthly payments are less. Leases generally last two or three years and then you return it and lease another vehicle. So you'll always be trading into the newest vehicle and you can change models every couple of years. Because you are leasing the vehicle, you are paying to use it—essentially, renting it. Therefore, since the leasing company gets the vehicle back to sell after your lease is complete, your payments are usually much less.

This is good for those who would like to get into a new car but don't have a lot to spend. And sometimes it is also good for those who may be using it for business and need a reliable vehicle.

Now the downside of leasing. You will always have a payment and there is generally an annual mileage limit. For example, if you have a 12,000-mile annual mileage limit, any additional mileage over that will cost you more when you turn the vehicle back in. So if the over mileage charge is 35 cents per mile, and you drive an additional 2000 miles over the course of the lease, you will be paying an additional $700 at the end of the lease. This is just food for thought if you're someone who loves to be on the road a lot.

Another drawback to leasing is if you decide to purchase the vehicle at the end of the lease. Leasing companies will be selling the vehicle at fair market value to the buyer; this includes you. Therefore, although you've made the required leasing payments for the past two or three years, you will be paying far more for that same vehicle over the course of the lease and purchase than if you purchased it in the first place. Switching from a leasing scenario to a purchase is not necessarily good or bad; the purpose of all of this information is so that you the consumer can make an informed decision before you get into a lease. Many who lease with the intention of buying the vehicle after the lease has ended think that they will be getting a great deal when it comes time to purchase that vehicle. When the lease is over however, they are shocked to learn the purchase price of the vehicle that they have been driving and caring for the past few years. When I was younger, I personally experienced this and I've heard countless stories from others having the same experience over the years. In the end, most would rather pay a little more on a term loan and own the vehicle outright when the loan is paid off. Then the next few years will be payment free. If your plan is to keep the vehicle for an extended period of time, then in the long run this is the most cost-effective option.

New Car Warranties

When purchasing a new vehicle, the manufacturers will have a warranty that will cover certain repairs for a predetermined length of time or mileage, whichever comes first. It's important that you read your warranty information to see what is covered and what isn't. For example, most warranties are divided up into sections such as basic, drive train and corrosion warranties. In the warranty information there may also be information regarding roadside assistance.

There is a reason why we all need to be aware of what is included in our new car warranty. Every year, thousands take their vehicles to independent shops for certain repairs that they pay for when the repair could have been covered under the manufacturer's warranty, and not costing them a dime. Many times, I've sent customers to their local dealership for a warranty repair that they were prepared to pay hundreds of dollars for.

Here is another little tip: Although the manufacturer's warranty may be recently expired, if you have an ongoing issue with your vehicle, at times they will have a special policy regarding that specific failure or manufacturer's defect. In other words, if they know that there has been an issue with a specific part failure, at times they will extend the warranty to cover the repair for a specific period of time. This is not to be confused with a "safety recall," which is where the manufacturer voluntarily or is required to contact you to get a repair completed that is safety related, for example a repair to your restraint system or brakes. The special policy is something you may never even know exists unless you ask about it. So, if a system or part fails after your warranty is up, and it just doesn't seem like it should have that soon, call your tech or the dealer and ask about it. You'll lose nothing but a moment of your time, but it could save you hundreds and possibly thousands of dollars.

Aftermarket Warranties: Read the Fine Print

You may have seen ads on TV, or perhaps you've gotten some literature in the mail concerning extending your warranty or offer to sell you a new aftermarket warranty or protection plan. Use caution when purchasing these warranties, as many times what seems like a little security is nothing more that someone trying to take your money and offering very little help in return when the need arises.

If an aftermarket warranty is something that is offered to you when purchasing a used or certified pre-owned vehicle, ask if the warranty is affiliated with the manufacturer. Some manufacturers offer an extended warranty. These are usually pretty good if you decide to purchase one. The problem arises when the used car lot offers an aftermarket warranty from a third-party company not affiliated with the manufacturer.

Before purchasing, read the fine print very carefully. Many times, the warranty will cover only certain parts of the vehicle but not others. Now although this sounds reasonable, considering the many parts on a car that could fail, I have personally experienced situations where I had to apply some pressure (with mixed results) to the aftermarket warranty company because they claimed the part or repair involved was not covered by the warranty. Trying to collect can be another story: you're at the mercy of whomever you are speaking to on the other end of the telephone. Many aftermarket warranty companies don't like to pay out claims, and if they do, make it very difficult. Most independent shops will not deal with these warranty companies because of all the red tape; often, they won't pay the labor rate that the shop charges, so it's not worth it to the shop to do the job. In most situations, the repair shop will have the customer pay them for the repairs and then it will be up to you to collect from the warranty company. I'm not saying that all aftermarket third-party extended warranty companies are bad. However, if I'm going to make a recommendation, I would stay with one that is backed by the manufacturer and one that I know will still be there next year or three years from now.

Manufacturers offer extended warranties on used or pre-owned vehicles, but these warranties may be administered by another company. These warranties may be called by a different name like "protection plan" or "extended service agreement." For example, General Motors offers the General Motors Protection Plan (GMPP), which is administered and underwritten by member companies of GMAC Insurance Group; Ford offers Ford Protect and Chrysler offers Chrysler Warranty Direct. No matter who the manufacturer is, in most cases they offer an aftermarket warranty. The nice thing about these warranties is that, when taking your vehicle to the dealer for a covered repair, it's pretty cut and dried. It's almost as if the original warranty is still in effect, the only difference is that you purchased the extended warranty yourself at the time that you purchased your vehicle, or shortly thereafter. If you want a little peace of mind with your vehicle purchase then I recommend that you consider one of these programs. Again, before signing on the dotted line, go to the website of the warranty provider and read everything about the particular plan you are purchasing. Their websites will tell you the different levels of protection available and what is covered with each of the plans.

Extended warranties aren't for everyone. However, if the reader isn't prepared to pay for a large repair if it arises, then it may be a good investment for them. For those who are diligent about researching, seeking out reliable vehicles and doing the regular maintenances on time, then an extended warranty may not be of value or worth the money that they pay up front for it. Extended warranties are no different than any other type of insurance: it's a personal preference and it's something that may or may not be used.

Chapter 3: First Things First, Before You Get Behind the Wheel

Yes, We Still Need Emergency Kits

Although today's cars and trucks are more reliable than ever before, on occasion, they do break down. Not only that, we can never predict when or where they are going to break down. This is why having an emergency kit in your vehicle is still a necessity. This is specifically true when you are taking a long trip. If you happen to have car troubles at night, you will want a bright flashlight. If it's January and you are in a northern climate, you will probably want a blanket. Most likely you will be calling a roadside assistance company for help. But depending on several factors, they may arrive on the scene anywhere from fifteen minutes to a few hours later, so you should be prepared for the worst.

While most kits will include a lot of the same items, depending upon where you live there will be some other items you may want to add to your kit. Here is a basic list of items to put in your kit.

- A good First-aid kit
- A 2lb dry powder, class A, B & C fire extinguisher
- Three reflective triangles (should be placed fifty feet apart)
- Tire gauge

- Jumper cables: I recommend a good quality cable set, a minimum of sixteen feet long and 6 gauge. The higher the gauge number the thinner the cables are, so 6 gauge as a minimum or even 4 or 2 gauge are even better. Check out the Coleman Cable 08660 booster cable
- A good quality flashlight with extra batteries
- Gloves
- Rags
- A roll of duct tape (this saved me once when a radiator hose blew!)
- A small tool kit including a pair of pliers, Phillips and flat screwdrivers, a dead blow hammer and assortment of fuses
- Drinking water
- Non-perishable snacks

If it gets cold where you're at or traveling to, I would recommend that you put a warm blanket, a small shovel and some kitty litter in your vehicle. The kitty litter is to help your vehicle regain traction if you are stuck. Shovel as much snow as possible and then sprinkle the kitty litter in the path that the drive tires will take.

Last but not least, the item that you probably keep with you every day, your cell phone. Make sure that it has a full charge and that you have a charger that plugs into the accessory plug of your vehicle. A dead phone doesn't do you much good and you may need to make multiple calls.

Where's Your Owner's Manual?

Do you know where your owner's manual is? Many times your technician will go to the glove box or storage compartment and find no owner's manual in the vehicle. The manual doesn't do any good if it is sitting in the closet at home or under a pile of newspapers on an end table. On some vehicles, it is the quickest source or even the only thing that shows you where the battery is (no, they aren't always under the hood). On many vehicles, the owner's manual is the only road map to tell what all those fuses are used for. Most reputable repair facilities should have a good online or computerized service manual, but sometimes a tech will go directly to the owner's manual to find certain basic information like which fuse controls the accessory outlet or door locks. At times, the online service manuals can give a tech information overload and it is quicker to go directly to the owner's manual. A quicker repair time translates into you saving money—now we're talking.

The information contained in the owner's manual can prove to be critically important when needed; so if you bought your vehicle used, and it didn't come with an owner's manual, then purchase one from the dealer or online. Keep your owner's manual in your glove box or storage compartment so that it is there if you or someone helping you needs it.

What's Under the Hood?

Before you get behind the wheel, open the hood and check the fluid levels and condition. If you have never done this before, checking the fluids can seem a bit intimidating, but it really isn't; you can do this! Do you remember that owner's manual that's sitting in your vehicle's storage compartment? Most owner manuals will show you how to check basic fluid levels. If you still are unsure of how to do it or (ahem) you can't find your owner's manual, most of us have the internet readily available and there are a few websites on the web that can help with tutorials. www.carcarekiosk.com is a good place to start. Although I don't endorse everything on the site, they do have some very good information.

Check the Oil, Check the Oil, Check the Oil . . .

Twenty-five percent of vehicles on the road do not have the proper oil levels. On average, we get at least one or two vehicles, every day, that come in that are very low on oil, and some have no oil showing on the dipstick at all. These customers come in for other services like brake inspections or an alignment, and it is during our courtesy inspection that we check their oil level.

Today's vehicles are more reliable than years ago, and this has made a lot of us become more complacent when it comes to checking our fluids, especially the oil. Part of the reason is because, with the advancement of modern lubricants, particularly motor oil, auto manufacturers are going longer between oil changes than ever before. Many of us in the repair industry are of the opinion that this is not necessarily a good thing. Here's why.

Today vehicles are made with much tighter tolerances. The horsepower that is produced by some turbo charged four-cylinder engines can rival the V8 engines of the past. They tend to run hotter than the engines of the past, which, paired with precision sensors, control modules and actuators, allow today's vehicles to run much more efficiently and longer. Improved reliability comes at a cost, however. The hotter temperatures and tighter tolerances break down conventional motor oils more quickly, so it is especially critical to keep an eye on the level and the condition of the motor oil in your vehicle. Many new vehicle manufacturers have now gone to synthetic motor oil to help fight premature oil breakdown and possible premature engine failure. With these synthetic motor oils, it is possible to go longer between oil changes, but caution should be exercised when doing so: proper levels still should be checked frequently and adhered to.

Keeping an Eye on Your Fluids: It's Easier Than You Think!

Years ago, part of the process of filling your tank with gasoline was popping the hood and checking the fluid levels. This was, for the most part, an automatic service when filling up at a full-service gas station. This service helped drivers keep their critical fluids topped off and the engine running smoothly. Today however, full-service gas stations are passé and we as motorists have the responsibility of checking our own fluids. This is where the complacency comes in. We are a busy society; we don't make time for that sort of thing. When it comes to checking under the hood, it went from full-service to self-service to no service of today. How often do you see anybody getting fuel, open the hood of their car or truck and check the fluids anymore? I dare say rarely, if at all. What was once a common practice occurs infrequently at the gas pump today.

With all of the technological advances in the automotive industry, vehicles still need their fluids checked. Nevertheless, because they aren't checked, vehicles that could easily go for 200,000 or 300,000 miles are cut short. Let's face it, technology only goes so far: you as the car owner have to do the rest—checking or having your fluids checked frequently, scheduling regular maintenance, etc.

Five minutes could save you thousands of dollars. Okay, so I gave everybody the benefit of the doubt, it probably only takes about two or three minutes to check your vehicle's fluids. But those critical two or three minutes could mean the difference between just having a two-dollar hose clamp replaced, or a 4000-dollar (or more) engine job done. Here is what happens when your car or truck runs low on these crucial fluids.

- Engine oil: This is the lifeblood of the engine. If this level gets too low it is almost certain that your vehicle's engine

will suffer from catastrophic failure requiring major engine repairs or replacement.
- Engine coolant: This is what keeps your engine from overheating in the summer and gives you heat in the winter. Like sweat evaporation helps keep you cool on a hot day, the engine's coolant allows excessive heat to be transferred from the engine to the radiator where it is then dissipated. If the coolant gets too low and the engine overheats for a specific amount of time, it too can cause catastrophic failure to the engine. Hybrid vehicles often have a separate coolant reservoir for the generator/motor in the transmission, so don't forget to check the level for this also.
- Automatic transmission fluid: This fluid is vital for your car's transmission to function properly. Without this fluid, the automatic transmission cannot transfer the energy produced by the engine to the drive axles and ultimately to the drive wheels. If the transmission fluid gets low, the transmission will not shift properly or may be jerky. Again, gone for too long will most likely result in major transmission repairs just around the corner.
- Brake fluid: When you press the brake pedal, brake fluid is transferred from the master cylinder to a hydraulic cylinder at each of the wheels. Whether your car has disc or drum brakes doesn't matter at this point, what is important is that that brake fluid does not get too low. Now the brake system should never get below the low mark. If it does, then the brake pads are getting very worn out and they are in need of replacement or the brake hydraulic system has a leak in it. Run too low on this fluid and your ability to stop will be greatly reduced. The first indication will be a spongy brake pedal or one that goes to the floor.
- Power steering fluid: Although hydraulic power steering is quickly being replaced by electronic steering, there are still many vehicles out there that still use a hydraulic power steering system. If you get low on this fluid, you will notice

that the steering will become extremely difficult, especially at slow speeds.

A Quick Look at Car Rentals—What?

Undoubtedly, at some point, your car will be going into the shop for repairs and you may be without your ride for more than a day. If this happens, do you have a way to get around? What's your contingency plan if you lose the use of your vehicle for a couple of days? Here is a way to be prepared for such a situation. If possible, save enough money for at least a minimum of three days' car rental and put it aside. Many times customers will come in for extensive repairs and they will insist that their vehicle be finished at a specific time of the day. Most repairs take time, and this time can be extended further due to corroded parts not coming apart or parts logistics—in other words, the local part store may have to order your part, which may take a day or two to get. Long story short, be prepared to be without your vehicle. Being proactive and putting a little money aside to cover a two- or three-day car rental is one way you will ensure that you won't be left without transportation and that the technician working on your car or truck is not having to rush through the job. Rushing your technician will not be to your advantage, as mistakes can occur when one is hurried through anything. Would you rush a surgeon who has your life in his hands?

Whenever renting a car, do an inspection for any scratches or dents or any obvious flaws. Check the fluids and fuel level and report anything you see that is wrong to the rental agent. When you return the vehicle, ensure that you've refueled it for the next person, otherwise the rental agency may charge you a premium price for refueling. One last bit of advice on rental cars: check with your normal auto insurance agent to see if they cover rental vehicles. If not, then it is worth the few extra dollars to purchase the extra rental insurance when renting the car. On top of your car's repair, the last thing you will want is to have to pay for any damage incurred to the rental vehicle while it's in your possession.

Chapter 4: Routine Maintenance

Get the Most Out of Your Purchase

You work hard for what you have, so it just makes good sense to take care of the car that you have paid for or may still be making payments on. In doing so, here are a few service items to remember to ensure that you get the most out of your vehicle purchase.

At the risk of sounding repetitive, as I mentioned in Chapter 3, check your fluids. This is probably the single most common cause of premature failure for the engine or transmission. Proper levels of high quality fluids will help keep your vehicle going much longer than those that never get checked or changed. When the fluids get dirty or contaminated they should be replaced with fresh. This is why manufacturers have maintenance schedules, which include fluid changes to prevent them from becoming very dirty or contaminated.

Fueling Up: Does It Really Make a Difference?

Most car owners don't consider the importance of a good quality fuel. I once had a customer who brought his GMC Canyon to my shop for a misfire. Upon completing his diagnostics, my tech showed me the two partially plugged fuel injectors that came off the engine. While on his way home from a trip, the customer fueled up at a small gas station. It wasn't long before he started to notice the occasional misfire in the engine; by the time he pulled into his driveway, the misfire was consistent. As we were looking at his injectors, my customer asked what to look for and why it makes a difference from one station to another. I recommended using a high-volume gas station.

Gasoline is not like oil, it is highly refined. It also has additives mixed in with it to help keep your fuel system, like fuel injectors, clean. One of gasoline's characteristics is volatility; this is how well it vaporizes. Gas needs to vaporize to ignite and burn in your car's engine. When gasoline is stored for extended periods in underground tanks, it can collect moisture and contaminants. In addition, as it sits in the tanks, the temperature goes up and down with the seasons, causing it to lose some of its volatility. As a result, when you pump this older fuel that's been sitting in the tanks into your vehicle, you are getting a lower quality and possibly contaminated fuel. The busier the station, the quicker the turnover in gas, and therefore the fresher the gas is likely to be.

Most fuels are okay, and if you generally fill up around home or work, you will most likely use the same stations. I generally fill up at one of three stations, and all of them are busy gas stations, having fuel delivered every few days. While on a road trip, stick to the bigger stations or truck stops. Avoid the little stations that are in the middle of nowhere. Although they may have fuel that is fine, you don't want to put them to the test while you're 300 miles away from home.

I once owned a 1994 Cadillac Deville. This particular vehicle required that I put 92 octane premium fuel in it to run smoothly. One occasion I filled up at a particular station that I had not used frequently before. A day later the engine started to labor and "ping." As soon as I was able to fill up again, I got fuel from my regular station, and the ping went away. Chalking it up to a bad batch of gas, a few months later I went back to that same station again to fuel. Again, the engine started laboring and the ping returned. I later found that the station owner had been accused of "watering" down the fuel. This is why it does make a difference where you get your fuel.

Do you own a Flex-Fuel vehicle? If you aren't sure, just look for the yellow fuel filler cap or a yellow ring where you insert the gas nozzle if it is a cap-less fuel filler. Flex-Fuel vehicles can run on both gasoline or E85 gas-ethanol blended fuels. Here are a couple of things to remember when using E85 in your Flex-Fuel vehicle. Again, these recommendations are the result of compilations of my own experiences and those with whom I've worked with in the field.

- When switching from gasoline to E85, do it gradually. In other words, don't wait until your fuel tank is empty before switching from gasoline to E85 or visa-versa. Start switching when you still have approximately a half of a tank remaining. This gives your vehicle's sensors and control modules time to make the appropriate adjustments it needs to run smoothly.
- Here's another tip for those who live up in the northern climates: it is very important to replace your vehicle's spark plugs before they get worn out. E85 typically has less energy than gasoline. With worn-out spark plugs and in a colder winter climate, I have witnessed more fuel flooding situations resulting in a vehicle's not starting. This is easy to prevent however by ensuring that your spark plugs are replaced at the proper interval.

Here is my last point on fueling up. Many like to procrastinate when filling up their tanks, but there is a drawback to this. In today's vehicles, the fuel pumps are located in the fuel tank. There are two main benefits to this. First, it is the most efficient way of delivering fuel to the engine. Secondly, the fuel helps to cool the fuel pump, extending its life. By consistently running low on fuel, you stand a chance of shortening the life of your fuel pump. I generally try not to let my fuel gauge go below a quarter of a tank. In addition, by filling up before getting too low on fuel, you can afford to be a little fussier on fuel brand and price.

Lube, Oil & Filter: Same Thing, Only Different

One of the more common maintenance items that you, as a car owner, will encounter is getting an LOF, or Lube, Oil and Filter done on your vehicle. This is an important service that shouldn't be neglected, and if completed at regular intervals will greatly extend the life of your vehicle. The properties of motor oil have vastly improved over the years; they do a much better job of protecting your engine's vital internal parts in various climates. Motor oils of yesterday were more prone to sludge up quicker if not changed frequently.

The American Petroleum Institute, or API, certifies oil. On a bottle of motor oil you will see an API rating. I will provide a simple, non-technical explanation of this in the following paragraphs. If you would like to get into it a little deeper, I would suggest that you go to www.api.org. This website explains the API certification system, and it has some very interesting data if your curiosity pushes you to learn more.

Today, when you go to get the oil changed on your car or truck, you may be asked what type of oil you would like to use. All motor oils essentially do the same thing: lubricate. They are the same thing, only different. The three types of motor oil that are generally used in vehicles are conventional, synthetic and a synthetic blend. In layman's terms, conventional oil is good, synthetic blends are better and full synthetic oil is best.

This is a touchy subject with some drivers or techs and you may have heard opinions like, "Once a vehicle is using conventional motor oil or synthetic, don't switch between the two or your car will start leaking." Rest assured, with today's refined motor oils, if your vehicle starts leaking oil, is was going to leak regardless of whether or not you used conventional or synthetic motor oil. Several years ago, when this debate was in full swing, I personally switched between the two with no ill effects—my car didn't start gushing oil out of its seals or gaskets. But, to be on the safe side, don't switch back and forth. Pick one and stick with it.

Now with that out of the way, the condition of your car will determine what type of oil I would recommend. However, I will keep this simple: if your car or truck is close to being retired or is a leaker, then use conventional motor oil. The reason for this is that the synthetic oil is two to three times as expensive as conventional motor oil and if its leaking out or your vehicle is worn out, you will be throwing your money away. Keep conventional or synthetic blend in it and run it until it is time to trade the vehicle in. On the other hand, if your vehicle is in good condition, newer and you plan on keeping it as long as possible, then I would recommend using full synthetic oil. As mentioned earlier, many manufacturers have started manufacturing vehicles using synthetic oil and recommend synthetic when getting the oil changed. Synthetic oils are particularly good in hot or cold climates, as they don't tend to thin out or gel up like conventional oil does. So on those very cold mornings, when you go out to start up your car or truck, that oil is immediately pumped to the vital parts of your car's engine, protecting it from excessive wear. Conventional oils may take a few seconds to get moving and make it to where it needs to go. In hotter climates, synthetic oil doesn't thin out the same as conventional oil, due to the excessive heat, again protecting your engine from excessive wear.

Now that you know a little bit about the difference in oils, although I have made some recommendations, first and foremost, read your owner's manual. If your owner's manual recommends synthetic oil then use it, don't use conventional or blends. If you do, you may very well be digging an early grave for your engine. The only aspect on which I'd depart from the manual on is if it recommends conventional motor oil, you won't hurt it if you use synthetic or a synthetic blend. In fact you may even extend the life of your vehicle!

Belts and Hoses

While getting your oil changed, two things that should be inspected are the belts and hoses. With the advancement of materials from which they are made that allow them to last longer, often these two items are overlooked.

Today's engines run hot for the best performance and fuel economy. Therefore, it is critical that your car's cooling system be inspected and the hoses replaced when necessary. When a cooling system hose gets a hole in it or blows open, it's just a matter of seconds before all of the coolant drains out and the engine will overheat.

Years ago, vehicles would have the alternator driven by its own belt, while the power steering and air conditioning compressor would also have their own drive belts. If one of these belts broke, generally the other belts would still be intact. One of these belts also ran the water pump, which circulates the coolant, keeping your engine from overheating. Today, on most cars and trucks, there is only one accessory drive belt, sometimes called a serpentine belt. If this serpentine belt breaks, everything that is run by the belt ceases to operate. This means the alternator stops charging, the air conditioning stops cooling, the water pump can't circulate that coolant, and if your vehicle has a power steering pump, you will lose any steering assist and the steering will become very difficult. So essentially, you will be calling a tow truck.

With so much depending on the integrity of your vehicle's belts and hoses, the importance of having them inspected and replaced when necessary is clear. If your technician or service writer doesn't mention it to you, then ask them to inspect and replace them when necessary. This is especially true for vehicles five years old or older.

Don't Forget About the Blades

Many overlook this simple but very important item until they are unable to see out of the windshield and driving becomes hazardous. Every time you get your oil changed, if they don't already do it during the courtesy inspection, have your tech check your wiper blades and replace them if necessary. Wiper blades wear out quickly, especially the cheaper blades, which only last me about three months, so replacing them every six months or so is not unusual. The signs that your wiper blades need to be replaced is that they "chatter" across the windshield when in use. Or, they may cause streaking on your windshield. One of the times that having good windshield wipers is very crucial is when it isn't even raining. Have you ever gone out, first thing in the morning with dew on your windshield, and you have to drive in the direction of the rising sun? It's difficult to drive facing into the sun, but when your wipers are worn, it then goes from being difficult to extremely hazardous. You aren't able to see the edges of the road or the oncoming traffic. Sometimes cleaning the wipers with a soft cloth and glass cleaner will get you a few more days out of them, but generally you'll be due for new blades soon.

Several types of wiper blades are available. The traditional (cheap) wiper blades don't work well in climates that get snow or ice, as they will freeze up, rendering them virtually unusable. Snow blades are available for the winter months. These have a rubber-like covering to keep the snow and ice from getting lodged in the metal framework of the traditional wiper blade. Then there are the more advanced "curved" style wiper blades. These are usually more expensive than the traditional wiper blades but will last longer and, because of the design, the wiper tends to stay in contact with the windshield better. These are my wiper blade of choice, particularly the Bosch curved blades such as the ICON or Evolution, I can generally get about a year out of them.

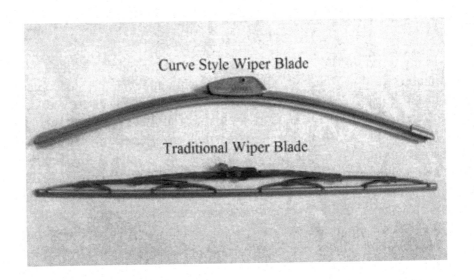

Tires Work Great Under Pressure: Keep Them Inflated and Rotated

Tires come in a variety of styles manufactured by several different companies. Most tires on the market will serve you well as long as you keep them inflated and rotated. Again, this service is one that should be completed regularly but is often neglected.

Modern tire pressure monitoring systems (or TPMS) have made it much easier to continually monitor your tire pressures. Proper tire pressures will help your pocket book by allowing you to get the fuel economy that your vehicle was designed to get. Underinflated tires cause your fuel economy to suffer. According to www.fueleconomy.gov, "you can improve your fuel economy by up to 3.3% by keeping your tires inflated to the proper pressure." Although this doesn't sound like a lot, it can add up fast over the course of the year, depending on how much driving you do. Adding that to the savings in tire costs, you'll see that it's worth keeping an eye on your vehicle's tire pressures.

Tire inspection and rotation should be done whenever you get the oil changed in your vehicle. Here is the reason why: The average tire makes approximately 800 revolutions for every mile traveled. During those 800 revolutions, your tires hit potholes, road kill and debris in the roadway. Tires take a tremendous amount of abuse and are expected to perform for several thousand miles.

Think about it. No other part of your car goes through more abuse than your tires; your brakes or suspension system would come in a close second. This is why I recommend having the pressures checked and having your tires rotated and inspected regularly to catch any excessive wear patterns that may be an indication of worn suspension parts. Also during tire inspections, debris like nails or screws can be removed and the tire patched, again allowing you to get the full life out of the tire and saving you money!

Wheel rims are prone to start leaking as they age; this is especially true with aluminum rims. The reason this happens is that corrosion starts to build up where the tire seals to the rim, causing the tire to start losing air. If caught early enough, the tire can be dismounted from the rim and the corrosion is then removed; the tire is then resealed to the rim and you're back on your way. However, if this condition is left without being corrected, the tire pressure can drop down to the point that permanent damage can occur to the tire and drastically shorten its life.

Before we move on to your brakes, let me make one last point. When your technician informs you that your tires are getting worn out and that they should be replaced, take his advice. There's a lot riding on your tires, particularly in the passenger seats. Let's say your car weighs approximately 3,500 pounds, which means that you're guiding a 3,500-pound missile down the highway at 60 or 70 mph. Having good tread on your tires could be the difference from stopping during inclement weather or plowing into the back of an already stopped vehicle in front of you. Or, the difference from skidding off into a ditch and guiding your vehicle around some debris in the road way.

There are many, many tire brands out there to choose from. The only truly bad tire is the bald tire with no tread on it. When it comes to shopping and purchasing tires, I have my own personal favorites, but there are so many good tires to choose from. Ask your technician what he recommends for your vehicle and your style of driving. Many dedicated tire stores can help guide you to the right tire as well.

Stop!

By now, you probably are aware that I am a huge advocate of safety. As a young man, I was a bit more carefree and perhaps a little too reckless. However, as we get a little older, and hopefully a little more mature, we tend to take our safety and the safety of our loved ones a little more seriously. The ability to bring that 3,500-pound (or more) vehicle to a complete stop is critical.

Like the tires, your braking system goes through a lot of abuse. The constant starting and stopping, heating up (from friction) and cooling down takes its toll over time. When braking, the brake fluid pressures in the metal lines get extremely high. The amount of pressure exerted on the brake rotors or drums, during sudden stopping situations, is very intense.

The purpose of this section on brakes is not to make you a brake expert in ten minutes or less. It is to express the importance of maintaining your vehicle's braking systems. To most of you reading this it may seem like a no-brainer, but you would be amazed—or rather shocked—to find out the condition of the braking system on many of the vehicles traveling the same roadways that you or your children are traveling.

Here is a quick simplified lesson on how most braking systems work. The main components are the master cylinder (to provide the brake fluid pressure), brake lines (to carry the brake fluid), calipers/wheel cylinders (to exert pressure on the brake rotor or drum via a brake pad or brake shoe). So, when you press on the brake pedal, fluid is forced out of the master cylinder through the brake lines and into the calipers if it has disc brakes, or into the wheel cylinders if it has drum brakes (nowadays, if drum brakes are used, they will only be used on the rear brakes).

If any one of those vital parts of the braking system fails, your ability to stop may be greatly reduced, or the brake system as a whole could fail to stop your vehicle. This makes it clear that brake inspections are critical and some states or areas may require them during annual inspections.

If your brake pedal goes all of the way to the floor, you most likely have brake fluid leaking somewhere, or on the rare occasion the master cylinder may have failed. In any event, don't drive your car, but have it towed to your repair shop instead. While braking, if you hear a grinding noise coming from any one of your wheels, get your vehicle to your shop as soon as possible. This means that the brake pad material itself has most likely worn down to the metal mounting surface. It doesn't matter what the type of brakes, disc or drum, when the pad material is used up, there's nothing left but metal, and metal against metal doesn't make a good braking system.

Regular brake system inspections can help you avoid some of these situations. By closely monitoring the brake pad thickness, the necessary repairs can be performed BEFORE they are completely worn out and grinding. On older vehicles, the occasional brake line inspection should be performed; in northern climates, brake lines are prone to corrosion, which leads to brake fluid leaks and the eventual loss of your vehicle's ability to stop all together.

By performing this inexpensive routine maintenance, you could save hundreds of dollars by having only the necessary parts replaced when they are due. By waiting, the costs of the repairs will most certainly go up, as other parts like calipers or wheel cylinders may need to be replaced due to overheating or over-extending.

One last thing: when it comes to your brakes, don't cut corners. Brakes are a normal wear item, so expect to have them replaced or worked on occasionally. In addition, for the best braking performance, when your vehicle's brake pads are due to be replaced, the brake rotors or drums should be replaced as well.

Shocks, Struts and Other Suspension Stuff

The suspension of your vehicle consists of the parts necessary to keep your car's tires firmly planted on the road while driving. These consist of:

- *Shocks and struts*, which absorb the shock of hitting bumps or potholes in the road to help minimize the damaging effects of these vibrations from going through the chassis or other parts of the car.

- *Ball joints and tie rods*, which are pivot points that give your car the ability to steer (tie rods and ball joints) and allow the tires to have movement up and down, via the steering knuckle, when hitting those bumps or potholes (ball joints). A stabilizer bar, sometimes called a sway bar, stabilizes your vehicle while turning or while you're driving over uneven roads. There are "links" that usually connect both ends of the stabilizer bar to the strut or control arm on either side of your vehicle.

One other item needs to be mentioned: wheel bearings. They connect your car's suspension parts to the wheels and allow the wheels to rotate. Years ago, these used to be serviceable, in other words they could be cleaned, re-greased and re-installed. Today the majority of wheel bearings are sealed and cannot be serviced. Like the tires, the wheel bearings go through an extreme amount of abuse and eventually will wear out and require replacing. A common symptom is a whirring sound coming from the wheel area. It can be compared to the sound that a prop on an airplane makes. When you hear this sound, it may be a wheel bearing, and if so it will need to be replaced soon. If ignored, eventually the wheel bearings will become loose and cause excessive tire wear.

The previous two paragraphs gave a very basic description of the main steering and suspension parts that you will eventually hear your technician talk about. This is by no means a complete list. These are the most common components of your suspension system that wear out and will eventually need to be replaced if you intend to keep your vehicle for any extended period. So, if you notice a single "popping" noise when coming to a stop, this may be an indication that your car's ball joints are becoming worn out and loose. On the other hand, if your steering feels loose, causing you to have to over-correct, then this may indicate that your car's tie rods are wearing out and becoming loose. If, while going over small bumps, you hear a noticeable "rattle" sound coming from under your car, this could be due to worn or broken stabilizer bar links. A rattle while going over bumps can also identify worn struts, but they tend to have a deeper pitched sound to them. Weak shocks or struts will allow your vehicle to bounce while going over bumps in the road. When they are completely worn out, your vehicle may bounce so violently that it can be difficult to keep it on the road. As a courtesy, your technician may inspect your struts and if they are leaking fluid may recommend replacing them. It is a good practice to have your tech do a suspension inspection while changing your vehicle's oil. This will allow them to find any small problems before they become big ones, like broken ball joints or tie rods.

Tires, Brakes and Suspension All Work Together As a Team...

Okay, we've discussed tires, brakes, wheel bearings and suspension parts; now what do they all have in common? The answer is that these parts of your car absolutely rely on each other to keep the rest of the vehicle on the road, and to keep you safe. If your tires are bald and have no tread then the brakes can't do their job effectively. If the suspension is weak or worn out then the brakes and tires can't do their job. If the brakes are not working properly then the suspension will not perform efficiently. Get the picture? These systems work together in order to keep your car on the road. Your brakes enable your car to stop, good shocks and struts help your car to stop quicker and several feet shorter. Therefore, when your tech tells you that your car will need brakes, wheel bearings or struts soon, plan on it. If these common wear items are replaced when they are due, your repair bill will be a little easier to digest. Repair bills will escalate if you procrastinate: before you know it your car will need ball joints, tie rods, wheel bearings and brakes, all at the same time, and the repair bill will easily go into the thousands of dollars.

Do I Really Need a "Tune-up"?

Years ago, a tune-up consisted of replacing spark plugs, ignition wires, distributor cap and rotor. If you went back even further, the tech would also replace the points, condenser and set the dwell and timing. Perhaps the air filter and fuel filter would be changed and carburetor adjustments were made if needed.

Okay, I've read articles where some techs get all bent out of shape for using the term "tune-up" when it's not really a tune-up in the old sense of the term. Do you really need a tune-up? Probably not, since about the only thing that gets replaced anymore are the spark plugs and the occasional fuel filter. Some of us old timers, and certain labor guides, may call it a tune-up out of habit. If your technician happens to tell you, "It's time for a tune-up," ask them what they are talking about. What are they replacing?

The advancement of automotive technology has all but eliminated the need for the traditional tune-up. Where years ago, the distributor provided for the mechanical timing and distribution of ignition spark, the computer systems of today provide the ignition timing through the use of camshaft and crankshaft sensors; eliminating the distributor all together. Therefore, there is no more need to replace the distributor cap, rotor, points or condenser, and with coil over spark plug technology, no more spark plug wires!

Some of you more seasoned drivers may remember getting tune-ups or the timing and dwell checked every 15,000 to 30,000 miles, sometimes even less if your vehicle was running poorly. With the elimination of all of these mechanical timing parts and improvements in computer and spark plug technologies, servicing your car's ignition system (i.e. replacing the spark plugs) only needs to be done approximately every 100,000 miles. (Smiley face)

However, on some vehicles, unfortunately there is a down side to this. Because vehicles can go longer on a set of platinum or iridium spark plugs, manufactures have designed some engines that take more time to get to the spark plugs. In other words, other parts may need to be removed to gain access to the spark plugs. So again, don't be surprised when your tech tells you that it's going to take two or three hours, and cost $300 to $400 or more, to replace your vehicle's spark plugs. Just remember, this may be the only time that you'll ever need to do this while you own the car.

80,000 to 100,000 Miles: The Ever-important Timing Belt

Vehicle manufacturers vary in their recommendations for timing belt replacement intervals, but the general rule of thumb is between 80,000 and 100,000 miles. Not every vehicle has a timing belt, however; some have timing chains, which do not need to be replaced at the same interval as the timing belt, if ever—the owner's manual or your tech can help you with this. Take a few minutes to find out if your vehicle has a timing belt or a chain.

Briefly, the timing belt, or chain, is what keeps the valve train (where the air comes into the engine and the exhaust out of the engine) and the pistons (which compress the fuel and air mixture) in time with each other.

Generally speaking, timing belt replacement is a rather straight forward process on many vehicles that your technician can take care of for you. However, some engines may require special tools or procedures that your tech may send you to the dealership for. If this is the case for this procedure (or others), this is just them showing wisdom and common sense, so be very thankful. I've seen some, including techs, get in over their heads by not knowing their own limitations. Sometimes, it can be a big job that may be better off completed at the dealership where they have all of the specialized tools, training and experience.

Some shops may only see a particular make and model vehicle come in for a scheduled timing belt replacement or timing chain issue once every two or three years—or perhaps ever—whereas the dealerships are working on that make of vehicle every day of the week. If you needed major surgery, would you want to go to your primary care physician or a specialist in that area who does that particular surgery every week? Again, most timing belts are straightforward and can be replaced by your technician. They will let you know of the complexity of the job and if they are comfortable doing it or if you should take your vehicle to the dealership.

One last thing on this subject: this is typically not a cheap service. Most timing belt jobs start at approximately $600 and go up from there to over $1000. The reason that they can get expensive is because usually, when replacing the timing belt, your tech may recommend replacing the water pump and timing belt tensioner and pulleys. Many water pumps are hidden behind the timing belt, so when you hit that 80,000 to 100,000 mile mark, they will most likely recommend replacing the pump while everything is taken apart and he or she is right there.

Throttle Body What?

With the advent of fuel injection, carburetors have fallen by the wayside. Fuel injection is a much more efficient way of providing fuel to your vehicle's engine, but without a carburetor how does your engine get air to burn the fuel? The new way is by using a device called a throttle body. In simple terms, your vehicle's computer uses this device to precisely control how much air the engine receives, at any given time, to provide the best fuel economy and power throughout various temperature ranges from sub-zero to over 100 degrees Fahrenheit.

Inside of the throttle body is a throttle plate, usually round. This plate pivots constantly, making small opening and closing adjustments inside of the round, tubular shaped throttle body. As your vehicle's computer monitors the airflow going into the engine via the Mass Air Flow (MAF) and Manifold Absolute Pressure (MAP) sensors, it makes constant corrections to the fuel and the throttle plate, allowing more or less air into the engine.

When your engine is idling, say at a stop light, the throttle plate is almost closed; only enough air gets through to keep the engine idling smoothly. When you accelerate away from the stop light, the fuel injectors allow more fuel into the engine, in turn the throttle body must quickly open to provide the air so that fuel can burn efficiently. The problem arises when the throttle body becomes gummed up with grime and tarry deposits. At idle, that small opening becomes restricted, not allowing enough air to keep the engine running, so it frequently stalls out at idle; or stalls when accelerating from a stop due to the throttle plate sticking and not opening smoothly when commanded by the computer. Sometimes, depending on the severity of the condition, this may flag a diagnostic code in the computer or PCM and cause the "check engine" or "Service Engine Soon" light to come on.

Throttle body service is crucial to the smooth operation of your vehicle, yet quite often it is overlooked. I would recommend that at approximately 50,000 miles, the throttle body should be cleaned. Some vehicles are more prone to this gumming up than others, and some throttle bodies are easy to get to while others are not, so ask your technician for their recommendation.

Now that you've passed Throttle Body 101, let's move on.

What Every Driver Should Know

Cleaning Fuel Injectors?

Okay, this section on fuel injectors will be brief. Some shops, including some dealerships, will encourage, and at times pressure you into getting your car's fuel injectors cleaned on a regular basis. Some may just call this an injector service. It has been my experience that this doesn't add any benefit unless the need arises. Simply put, most fuels have detergents in them to help keep your injectors and the upper portion of your engine clean, so regular fuel injector cleaning is, in my opinion and experience, rather redundant and unnecessary. As mentioned earlier in this chapter, be careful when choosing the gas station that you fuel up at. Generally, the only time that you may need your fuel injectors serviced, cleaned or replaced is if you get contaminated fuel, which may cause them to become restricted; or if an injector fails all together. Having said that, if your dealer recommends an injector cleaning procedure to help with performance issues, then by all means have them complete the service.

Cooling System Flush or Exchange

I'll get right to the point: dirty coolant restricts or plugs heater cores and radiators. Once again, this is a case where spending a few dollars every couple of years can save you hundreds if not thousands of dollars later. Your engine's coolant has NO filter, so whatever contaminants it collects as it does its job of keeping your engine from overheating will continue to circulate throughout the cooling system until they find a place to settle into. As your car's engine ages, small amounts of chemicals, metals and corrosion build-up and are carried around the engine, radiator and heater core within the coolant (or, as some call it, antifreeze, because it is added to water to help keep it from freezing in the winter).

Now, under normal circumstances, in newer vehicles, this isn't an issue. The problem arises when your vehicles start to age. These trace amounts of deposits begin to accumulate within the radiator or heater core. (The heater core is a miniature radiator that provides the source of the heat when you turn your heater on in the winter.) When enough of the deposits collect at the bottom of your radiator or heater core, two things happen. If the radiator becomes too restricted from these deposits, engine overheating will most likely be the end result. The first sign that your heater core is getting restricted is when you go to turn on your heater. You'll feel the air moving but it won't be hot; it may be warm or lukewarm air at best. You may not notice this gradual process until it gets cold outside. When this happens, what can be done to correct it?

Ideally, regular coolant exchanges will help keep your vehicle's cooling system in top condition and running efficiently. A coolant exchange is simply that: the cooling system is drained of its coolant and fresh coolant is added. If restrictions in the radiator or heater core are caught early enough, they can be flushed out using flushing agents. Your technician can provide this service for you. If, however, nothing is done and the deposits become solidified, usually the only remedy is to replace the radiator or the heater core, which can be costly. When buying a used vehicle, it is very important that the coolant condition be checked. As mentioned in Chapter 2, the fluids should be translucent and not cloudy or dark.

Here is a tip for the do-it-yourselfers: when buying coolant to top off or add to your vehicle's reservoir (refer to your owner's manual), use the type of coolant that the vehicle's manufacturer recommends. You can generally purchase it by the gallon in full strength, which you must mix 50/50 with water. Or, for a little more money, you can purchase the 50/50 premixed coolant. It is best to purchase the premixed coolant. It's ready to go right into the coolant reservoir. By trying to save a few bucks and mixing your own using the full-strength antifreeze, 1) You stand the risk of not getting the correct 50/50 mixture, which could allow your engine's cooling system to freeze during the winter months.

2) By introducing water with heavy metals, minerals or chemicals into your cooling system, you could be inadvertently causing harm to the cooling system down the road.

Transmission Fluid

This too is often overlooked because the transmission fluid is only changed after a vehicle has been on the road for several thousand miles. On many vehicles, it's as simple as just draining the transmission fluid out and refilling it with fresh fluid. On others, it may be a little more involved because there may be a filter that may need to be replaced as well. Most newer vehicles use a synthetic transmission fluid that allows drivers to go longer between this service, but it is still critical to the life of your vehicle's transmission. These days, rebuilding or replacing the high-tech transmissions is much more expensive than the more standard transmissions of yesteryear, so take good care of the one you have and it will serve you well.

An important point to remember is this, when having your transmission fluid serviced, ensure that the technician is using genuine fluid approved by your vehicle's manufacturer. Generally, this means if you own a Honda, use Honda fluid. If you own a Volkswagen, use Volkswagen fluid. There have been instances with some vehicle makes and models where transmission issues have occurred after a service because the manufacturer did not approve the fluid. Therefore, when I service the transmission fluid, I use the manufacturer-approved fluid only; as the old saying goes, an ounce of prevention is worth a pound of cure.

Brake and Power Steering Fluid Service: Hmmm . . .

Like fuel injector service, these services may again be of limited benefit. Frequently, these are added services provided by the dealership. Are they unnecessary services? Not always. If your service technician offers these services, then discuss it with them. On older vehicles, a complete brake fluid exchange may not be possible due to the condition of the bleeder screws located in the brake assemblies at each of the four wheels. If the bleeder screw breaks before it can be opened, then additional work will need to be done. My experience has been that at some point after 100,000 miles, some of the hydraulic portions of the brake and power steering systems will begin to require replacing, and when this happens, the fluid will then be changed. Brake calipers begin to stick, steering gears or hoses will start to seep fluid to some degree. Where friction is involved, at some point, seals wear out and parts require replacing. Deal with the fluid exchange then.

Ultimately, the decision to perform certain services will be yours. Performing a power steering fluid or brake fluid service will certainly not hurt your vehicle, but as I mentioned, the benefits may be limited, and the cost of the service may be higher than would be justified by these. Be assured that if you keep your vehicle long enough, the brake calipers will need to be replaced or a power steering hose will start leaking and require replacing. At this point, the fluids will be exchanged during the repair process.

A/C Service: Some Like It Hot

For both of my sons, air conditioning is a waste; they like the hot weather and they would rather have the windows open. As for me, on a hot sticky summer day, you just can't beat air conditioning; I like my A/C.

Air conditioning is a fairly simple process of compressing the refrigerant (gas) using the compressor (pretty obvious, huh?). Then this high-pressure gas is cooled and condensed into a liquid by running through the (yup, you got it!) condenser (this is also where heat is expelled). Just before the evaporator, the liquid refrigerant is forced through a restriction in the line; in some cases through an orifice tube, in other cases through an expansion valve where it immediately turns back into gas (evaporates) and (right again, smarty-pants) through the evaporator, where the cooling effect takes place, heat is removed from the passenger area. And the cycle starts all over again.

Now this is an oversimplified description of what your air conditioning system does and how it does it. It also has a filter, called an accumulator or receiver/dryer and various sensors, but at this point this is all we need to know to navigate the repair business.

Many people are just fine with a climate control system that doesn't work and using the windows to cool down or move the hot air around. However, there is a downfall to not having a working air conditioning system, whether you use it to cool down or not. Most vehicles are engineered so that when the driver turns on the windshield defroster or defogger, the A/C compressor turns on. Here is the reason why…

When warm damp air hits cold glass, the moisture in the air condenses on to the surface of the glass, much like water droplets form on the surface of your glass of iced tea on a hot summer day. When the A/C is working, that moisture condenses onto the surface of the cold evaporator core, which is just above the freezing point. This condensed water then runs down and out of a drain tube to the exterior of your car.

So when you turn your defroster on, not only are you warming up your windshield using the warm air provided by the heater core, the moisture is removed from the air by the cooling effect of the evaporator. This is especially important when it's cold and raining outside and you want to warm it up inside.

I would therefore recommend that you have your air conditioning system serviced about every three years, or if you notice that it is not cooling as well as it used to. If you are having to recharge your A/C system every couple of months, then you have a leak somewhere in the system that needs to be addressed. When serviced, your technician should add some leak detecting dye to the system so that when you return (or sometimes the same day) they can find the leak much easier by looking for traces of the dye using a UV (ultraviolet) light. Since your A/C system is under high pressure, it can leak from anywhere, and this dye will help pinpoint exactly where the leak is so that it can be repaired.

READ THIS BEFORE ANY COMPRESSOR REPAIRS ARE DONE!

Okay, this is where parts supplier and repair shop, or text book and experience, may clash or part ways again. The purpose here is to help the reader save money on air conditioning repairs. After working for years in the shop, one thing I've learned is that aftermarket parts providers like to cover their behinds. Although they may not have a clue as to what is broken on your vehicle, if they can sell you extra parts to cover themselves, then they will. Here is an example…

Although A/C compressors can be purchased separately, many companies will attempt to sell an A/C compressor in a "kit." This kit comes with several items: obviously the compressor, an orifice or expansion valve, and accumulator (filter), flushing solution (to flush out the lines), PAG oil and sometimes a condenser. What's left? Maybe a few hoses and the evaporator? The reason why they do this is because they won't guarantee the compressor unless all of those items are replaced and the lines are flushed out. If the compressor suffers a catastrophic failure, then many times it will leave debris scattered throughout the A/C system. This is when flushing out the lines and replacing those other parts becomes necessary—this we all agree upon. Where we diverge is when the compressor clutch assembly fails.

The compressor clutch can fail without causing harm to the rest of the A/C system. In this case, the clutch alone can be replaced. In doing so, on many of today's vehicles the engine compartment is extremely tight on space, so many times the compressor has to be removed from the vehicle in order to perform this repair. Many of us who work on these systems every day would prefer to replace the entire compressor with a new unit while it is out. These vehicles are usually older with higher mileage, so if the customer is paying the labor to remove the compressor, and if the cost is not prohibitive, why not install a new compressor? In this case, just replacing the compressor, and also the accumulator (remember this acts as the filter and replacing a filter is a good thing) will suffice. Usually there is no need to replace the expansion valve, no need to flush out the lines, no need to replace the condenser. Also, when your tech removes the compressor, they can visually inspect for debris in the compressor or lines. This is ONLY when the compressor clutch fails. If there is reduced performance caused by a worn-out compressor or a restriction in the line somewhere, then further repairs and flushing will most likely be required. However, if the compressor clutch is all that has failed (which is common, by the way), then why pay potentially hundreds of dollars more in parts and labor when it's not necessary? Replace the compressor and accumulator and call it a day!

Don't Forget the Filters

The engine air filter is another one of those maintenance items that should be checked, but is often overlooked, during each oil change. Ask your technician to inspect this if it's not on his list of regular items to check. This is something that is almost always overlooked by the ten-minute lube places. Your engine's performance and fuel economy will benefit by replacing the air filter when it gets dirty. Performing this basic service will allow the engine to breathe the way it was engineered to.

Cabin Air Filter

Of all the additions that have been made to vehicles in recent years, this filter is probably one of the most beneficial to your health and comfort. The main job of this filter is to trap impurities, dust and pollen and keep them from recirculating through your vehicle's heating and air conditioning system. Simply put, it filters the air that you breath. This filter is also probably one of the most overlooked items on your car as well. By not replacing this regularly, you may notice a reduction in airflow when running your heater or air conditioner; worse yet, the air quality will suffer as well.

The condition of this cabin air filter is common... Ewww!

Is Your Car Ready for That Long Trip? Get a Pre-trip Inspection

You've been waiting and saving for that long summer trip; you've worked hard, put in the overtime and now you're packed and ready to go; but is your car ready? Many vacations or trips have been sidelined or delayed because the vehicle is not ready for the road.

When I was in the armed forces, a friend (for the purposes of discretion we'll call him Mark) and I were going on leave to his hometown in Ohio. We left late in the evening and were driving into the early hours of the morning when we heard the flopping noise of a tire that had gone flat. I said, "Well... let's get the tire changed and get back on the road!" We went back to grab the spare tire to discover that it too was flat. Ugh! About 2:00 AM, several miles from the nearest town and here we were, going nowhere. Don't forget, this was back in the late seventies, when cell phones were not yet an option for us. So we had to walk to the nearest town while trying to roll a flat tire along the way; this took several hours that we could have spent in Ohio.

Okay, the moral of this story is this: unless it's fairly new, or your tech has just gone over your car, get a pre-trip inspection done before your road trip. Had my friend Mark done this, his spare tire would have been ready to go. Incidentally, the spare tire is rarely checked and as a result is commonly underinflated or even flat. The reason Mark's spare was flat was that he had loaned his van to another friend. This friend had a flat tire, put the spare tire on and never got the flat tire repaired, or cared to tell Mark about it. Another moral: be careful who you loan your vehicle to!

Many times a pre-trip inspection can reveal worn brakes or suspension parts, or perhaps a leak that could leave you stranded somewhere. I recommend scheduling the inspection at least two weeks ahead of your planned departure day. This gives your tech the time to go over your vehicle thoroughly and make any necessary repairs that may be needed.

Moving On . . .

Okay, now you've gained a little appreciation and knowledge of some of the more commonly overlooked or neglected parts or systems on your vehicle and the importance of planned preventative maintenance to keep it on the road. Even with the best of maintenance, however, occasionally problems will arise: the "Check Engine" or "Service Engine Soon" light comes on, or it stalls out on you. What then? This could happen to any vehicle, old or new. Keep reading and we'll systematically work through it.

Throughout the auto industry, many parts of the modern automobile have abbreviations like MAF, MAP or CKP, for example. There are hundreds of these abbreviations that you may come across, or your tech may refer to when talking to you. To help you understand what these abbreviations mean or what part of your car they refer to, go to www.auto-dictionary.com

Chapter 5: Car Problems? Things You Should Know.

Breaking Down

It's something that nobody wants to experience but most do. You're driving along, going about your day and then it happens: your car starts chugging or the "Check Engine" light comes on. This happens to almost everybody at one time or another during their driving career. The first thing to remember is to relax and don't panic.

Cell phones have made having car problems a little bit more tolerable. Years ago, if your car broke down, you had pretty much two options: walk to the next town, or hitch-hike (the latter of which, however, I don't endorse for safety reasons). Today, help is just a phone call away—all the more reason not to panic. Here's what to do before the phone call...

- If your vehicle is still running, first get safely off the road.
- If your emergency flashers work, turn them on. This is to visually signal to other drivers to proceed with caution around you. This will also help the police and roadside assistance vehicles assist you, especially at night or when visibility is low.

- If it's safe to do so, get out of your vehicle and open the hood. This will let other drivers know immediately that you are having car trouble.
- Set up flares or other devices to warn other drivers. Again, as with the flashers, this will visually signal to others and assisting vehicles that you are stationary on the side of the road.

Back in Chapter 1, one of the recommendations given was to save the phone number of your roadside assistance company in your cell phone's contacts list, and this is why.

Although you have help at your fingertips, it's good to take note of what your car was doing when the check engine light came on or when your car broke down. This will help the tech who is working on your vehicle diagnose the problem quicker. Some problems are intermittent, so any information that you can pass on to the technician will be helpful. We seasoned techs know that breaking down is a stressful time for our customers. We will do everything within our power to get you back on the road again as soon as possible. You can help. Here's how.

Now, What's Your Car Doing?

Your technician or service writer will ask you a series of questions relating to what exactly is happening with your car. The more information that you can provide, the better! Take note of any noises or vibrations, anything that your vehicle is doing that is out of the ordinary. Are there any unusual smells, like the smell of gas, or perhaps an electrical burning smell? If you recently had repairs done by someone else, be sure to let them know. This may give them a place to start.

What's It Not Doing?

There are many things that your vehicle may not be doing, but for now we are just going to focus on a "not running" or a "no starting" condition on today's more modern vehicles. (Older classic cars will have their own set of possible causes, some similar to today's vehicles, and some not so much.) Here are the main symptoms that you need to tell your tech. Learn what these terms mean and be as specific as possible. "Died while driving," "crank no start" and "no crank." Many times a vehicle will be held up for days or misdiagnosed all because of lack of communication or a lack of understanding of what certain terms mean. This may seem obvious, but again you would be amazed at how often this happens. Using these terms and being as specific as possible will save you money and reduce the time you will be without your car. Many a time, a tech will end up in left field, on an intermittent condition, due to poor or insufficient information.

A note on intermittent conditions; If a condition is happening intermittently or occasionally, and your tech cannot duplicate the problem at that time, they may take a look at some basic things and tell you to bring it back when it occurs more frequently. This is especially true if there aren't any stored codes in the PCM (power train control module), no technical bulletins and no tech forum leads. As inconvenient as it may be, unless you are willing to pay for several hours of diagnostic time, it may be advantageous to you and save you money if you take it and return when the condition is more consistent. If you have a second vehicle, and you are willing to leave it for a few days, then that may be an option. Your tech will then be able to drive it to try to duplicate the concern while working on it in between other jobs.

Died while driving; This refers to any situation that causes your vehicle to die, or stall, while you are driving it. Note the conditions, highway speeds, and other potentially relevant factors. Were you stopped at a traffic light? How often does it stall? Does it start right back up? What's the frequency? Does this happen every time you drive or once every two weeks or more? If you are able to, note if the engine feels like it is running rough just before is stalls; in other words, do you feel the car shaking and then stall?

The cause of a vehicle to die while driving could be many things. That's why a proper diagnosis is essential, and only your technician can accurately do this with special test equipment. Although this book is not intended to diagnose your car for you, here are some of the most common causes of this condition that I've run across. A faulty fuel pump or charging system, or a faulty crankshaft and/or camshaft position sensor can cause this condition. A MAF, MAP or oxygen sensor that has failed can also cause this. And yes, we've had vehicles towed into the shop because they had run out of gas. If it only stalls when coming to a stop, this may be caused by a dirty or defective throttle body, or an EGR valve that is stuck open can also cause this condition.

Occasionally a vehicle will come to us on the back of a tow truck for a "died while driving" condition that is a result of low engine oil or coolant level. These are usually catastrophic, yet so easily preventable. So again, as mentioned in Chapter 3, keep an eye on that coolant and oil level!

These are just a few of the most common causes. There may be many more things that can be the root cause and sometimes it takes time for your technician to determine this and apply the correct fix.

Crank no start: This condition is when you attempt to start your car, you turn the key or push the button, and the engine turns over normally but the engine will not start and run on its own.

Some of the causes for a "crank no start" can be the same as with the "died while driving" scenario. The most common causes for this is a faulty fuel pump or part of the fuel delivery system. A faulty crankshaft or camshaft position sensor, MAF or MAP sensor, or a dirty or malfunctioning IAC valve may cause this as well.

Lest we forget, rodents (especially mice and chipmunks) love to chew on your vehicle's wiring, creating openings in electrical circuits. Squirrels and chipmunks love to chew through air filters, and store up for the winter by depositing nuts in your vehicle's air filter box. This will cause a "crank no start" condition, and at the very least will cause your vehicle to run poorly and probably cause the "check engine" light to come on. I once had a groundhog (some may call them woodchucks) climb up into the engine compartment of my pickup and proceed to chew through the wiring and even the braided fuel line. This caused a crank no start situation with the distinct smell of gasoline.

Again, this is not an exhaustive list of everything that could cause your no start condition, these are just a few of the most common causes that I have run across over the past few years.

No crank: This condition is when you attempt to start your vehicle and nothing happens. The starter doesn't engage and the engine does not turn over. If the engine cranks over really slowly, this could be considered a "no crank" condition as well. Sometimes the starter assembly may make a clicking noise that can be heard. If so, pass this information on to your technician or service writer.

The most common causes for this condition are a failed starter motor assembly, a weak or worn-out battery, or loose or broken battery cables or ground straps. An alternator that is not charging the battery properly can cause this condition as well. It may not have died or stalled on you while driving the day before, but the alternator may not have charged the battery enough to provide the large amount of power necessary for the starter to turn over your engine. If the battery is dead or weak, in extreme cases the headlights or dash lights will be dim or completely out.

What Every Driver Should Know

If you don't hear any clicking, look at your instrument cluster. Is there a "Security" light illuminated or flashing? If so, there may be a problem with the anti-theft system. If you have a second key or key fob, try it to see if the original key or fob is faulty. If it starts, then you've found your problem. As an important side note, *ALWAYS* keep a second, "known good" key or fob available. If you have only one to start your vehicle with, then go down to the dealership and get a second one made. Depending on the make and model of your car, the first thing that your tech or service writer will ask you for is that second key. If you don't have a second key, then they will have to get one made by a locksmith or the dealer; this may be much more expensive than if you have one made yourself and set aside.

If your car was running and starting the day or two before, and you go out to start it and everything is dead or at least dim—no headlights, dim or weak interior lights or dash lights—then your battery has most likely been run down by something. First check whether anything was left on, like your headlights. Or, check to see if there was a door or storage compartment that wasn't closed all of the way, causing a light-bulb to stay on. Make sure that no aftermarket accessories were left on overnight, GPSs, health care related accessories that may be plugged into the accessory outlet or cigarette lighter. If something was left on, it may be as simple as shutting it off or unplugging it and then recharging the battery for a minimum of two hours.

If you don't see that anything was left on overnight, then your battery may have what is called an "excessive parasitic drain," causing it to go dead rapidly. All vehicles have some sort of a parasitic drain; it's what keeps the memories stored in the entertainment system, or control modules while they are in their "sleep" mode. When a technician tests your vehicle for an excessive parasitic drain, he or she is looking for anything that is over the 50-milliamp threshold. Most modern vehicles are well below this: in their sleep mode, which may take 30 to 60 minutes to achieve, they may draw something well below 50 milliamps, even below 20, from the battery.

Now I know what you're probably thinking, "I'm not a technician!" Or, "Why is he telling me all about this technical jargon like milliwhatchamacallits?" The point I'm making here is that when your tech comes up to you and says that your car has a drain on the battery, you'll know exactly what they are talking about. A battery has only so much reserve power: the bigger the draw, the quicker it goes dead. Now the search begins to find out what is the source of the drain on your battery. Some parasitic drains can be found quickly and some not so much. Aftermarket accessories such as alarm, remote lock or remote starting systems can cause the battery to run down if not installed properly or if they fail.

While on the subject, beware of added on aftermarket alarm systems. Many aftermarket accessories can be a major problem if not installed correctly. I mentioned earlier that I'm not a big fan of aftermarket accessories, partly because most of the time they aren't installed properly and they involve tapping into the manufacturer's wiring harnesses. Although this may not sound like an issue, since the automobile manufacturer tries to seal all of their harness and connectors, breaking into that harness can create a place for moisture to intrude, causing corrosion that will result in broken wires and circuit failures in the future. They can also cause your technician to spend a lot more time diagnosing your concerns. In light of this, I believe that purchasing a vehicle with the factory installed accessories is more advantageous than trying to add the accessories after the purchase. Simply put, buy the car that you want, don't try to build the car that you want.

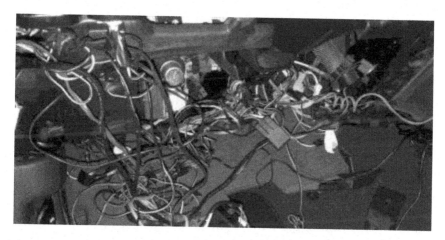

Aftermarket wiring nightmare.

Look and Listen to What Your Car Is Telling You

Frequently, your car can lead you to the problem area by the symptoms it has or the sounds that it makes. A check engine light on with a rough running engine could be a misfire condition—the engine isn't firing on all of the cylinders. If the "Check Engine" or "Service Engine Soon" light is flashing, this means there is a catalyst (catalytic convertor) damaging condition present that needs to be addressed immediately. As I mentioned in Chapter 4, if you hear a loud clunk coming from the front end when you are coming to a stop or taking off, you may have a worn or loose ball joint. As your vehicle ages and parts begin to wear or fail, there are very common sounds that techs listen for or symptoms that they are looking for. You too can learn to recognize and become familiar with some of these common symptoms.

Brakes and suspension are two of the most frequently performed services in the auto repair industry. This is why so many shops that specialize in just brake, suspension or exhaust repairs have sprung up over the years. If you think that you may have a problem with your brakes or your suspension, based on what your car is telling you, jump to the end of this book. Go to the heading "What's That Mean?": these are some of the most common automotive problems and the symptoms that go along with them.

One way that your car can communicate with you is through any one of its multiple control modules (computers). There are separate modules that control the engine, the transmission, antilock brakes, instrument cluster, radio, door locks, the windows—the list goes on and on. Although these modules can't scream out to you, "Hey buddy, yeah you sitting behind the wheel, I'm talking to you! My engine is misfiring on cylinder number three!" they do have their own language that anybody with an inexpensive scanner and a Smartphone can understand. Our cars communicate to us in the form of codes and data that can point us in the direction to go, maybe even allow us to correct the problem ourselves.

Recently I had a young college student stop by the shop on a Friday afternoon just before closing time. Her Toyota Celica had a check engine light on and was intermittently running rough. I plugged in my scan tool to see what her car was going to tell me. The Celica had a trouble code P0171 stored in the PCM (Powertrain Control Module). This code means that her engine is running "lean" on bank one. However, her car was running fine at the time; I did a quick check of the vacuum lines and hoses to see if there were any leaks, which could trigger this code. No leaks were visible and the connections looked and felt tight. I cleared the code and told her to drop it off if it came back on over the weekend and we would dig further into the problem. I also advised her that she might be looking at cleaning or replacing her MAF sensor.

The following Monday morning she came in beaming, smiling from ear to ear. She told me that she and her grandfather did a little homework on the internet over the weekend. Her grandfather suggested that she clean the MAF sensor; when she did, she found a very small "gross" (her word, not mine) bug lodged in the MAF sensor. After removing the "gross" bug and cleaning the sensor with MAF sensor cleaner, the car ran fine. She did still leave her car for me to clear the code again and test drive for her. She also wanted me to check over her car for her to see if anything else needed to be addressed.

This is a prime example of what any one of you can do to help save yourself some money. This young lady had very little knowledge when it came to car repair. Although vehicles have become more complex over the years, our web technology has kept up with it. Does this mean that you will be able to fix every problem that comes a long? Of course not, but many times I see customers paying $200, $300 or more for a car repair that is something that is very simple. If you have a good technician, work with them. The more you are willing to know the more they will be able to help you! Nothing pleases this tech more than seeing the light-bulb go on in a customer's head and hearing, "I get it, I understand!" or "I can do that!"

"There's a Light on! What's Wrong With My Car?"

Most of us are so familiar with our car or truck that they almost become an extension of ourselves. So when something, like a warning light, illuminates on the dash we immediately take notice. That itself can be scary if we weren't expecting it and our vehicle has never had a light on the dash illuminated before. The first thing to remember is to note which light is illuminated. Again, your technician or service writer will be asking for this information, so make a note of what light just came on and which lights have been on for a while.

Here is where you'll need to dig out the owner's manual that I told you about back in Chapter 3. Most owners' manuals will have a section in them that will display each of the warning lights and what they mean. This is very important because you don't want your tech spending too much time troubleshooting an intermittent light condition and chasing down the wrong light. Case in point...

This couple brings in a Chevy Impala in a frenzy: "Our check engine light is on!" they exclaimed. Worried about the costs of the repair, they take a seat in the waiting area. When the tech got the car in, he scanned the PCM for engine related codes, but none were present. He scanned the remaining modules and all came up with the same result, no codes. The only light that was lit on the dash was the low washer fluid indicator, so he went and brought the customers out to their car in the shop and asked them to point to the light that was lit during an initial bulb check. They immediately went to the low washer fluid indicator light and said, "There, that one!" A gallon of windshield washer fluid and they were back on their way. This was something that if they had looked in the owner's manual, they could have remedied themselves without having to sit in a waiting room worrying.

Okay, now that you've confirmed that it is in fact a "Check Engine" or "Service Engine Soon" (SES) light that is on, don't start worrying quite yet. Chances are that if your car is still running okay, you won't have to call a tow truck right away and you can drive to your repair shop. However, just because you don't notice any symptoms doesn't mean that you should ignore the warning light altogether.

Purchase a Scan Tool, Because Knowledge Is Power

Scan tools or code readers are a way for your car to communicate with you in a language that you can understand. Your car or truck may have certain symptoms and store certain diagnostic trouble codes in a control module in the form of computer code or electronic pulses; the scan tool takes that information and interprets and displays it so that us average humans can understand it. In so doing, we can see what system or component has failed or is about to fail.

Bi-directional scan tools are one of the most important and most used tools in a technician's tool box. Although their scan tools can be very expensive, over the years, more inexpensive user-friendly versions have come on to the market. Why do I bring this up? Because having your own inexpensive scanner or code reader at your disposal can help give you peace of mind.

Knowledge is power: the more you know going into the repair shop the more confidence you'll have. And again, when taking your car to your technician for repairs, any codes you can give him or the service writer will help streamline the repair process. For example, Check Engine or SES lights do not always stay on. Although there may be code(s) stored, conditions may be such that this light is no longer illuminated. If you notice a light coming on, do a quick scan and record the codes. This may help get your tech going in the correct direction and get you back on the road sooner.

Don't allow yourself to be intimidated by the prospect of using a scanner or code reader to communicate with your car. It's really pretty simple, the hardest part is plugging it into the on board diagnostics (OBD) connector. Not really: it's usually no further than about six inches away from either of your knees while sitting in the driver's seat. Some European vehicles may have it on the passenger side (go figure…).

The OBD connector looks like this.

BlueDriver Scan Tool for iPad, iPhone and Android Smart Phones

There are hundreds of scan tools on the market for the consumer. This can make it very confusing when purchasing one. Most do the same thing, but some a little better than others. Many online retailers like Amazon sell the scanners or code readers that I'm talking about.

- If you have an iPhone or Android smart phone, I recommend getting the BlueDriver scan tool. The BlueDriver is small and very user friendly. It can be used for just retrieving stored codes, or if you feel a little more adventurous and want to go a little deeper it has that capability as well. The BlueDriver sells for around $100 and the smart phone app is free. Go to www.lemurmonitors.com for more information about the BlueDriver.

- If you don't have a smart phone, you can still get an affordable scanner that is self-contained. These scanners won't be quite as compact, but they are manageable. Autel makes several affordable scanners or code readers, starting at about $20 and going up from there.

Although many of these are considered scanners, about the only thing most of you will want to use them for is to retrieve diagnostic trouble codes that your vehicle has stored in its control modules and relaying that information on to your technician. Some of them will give you the option to view live and freeze frame data and clear codes. Yes, I said that they can clear the stored codes. However, don't clear any codes unless your technician tells you to. If you clear the code, you may inadvertently remove any clues that your tech will have to find the underlying cause of your vehicle's problem. So just read the codes and write them down.

Your code reader or scan tool will give you a code that usually starts with a letter and ends in a four-digit number, for example P0302 or P0440. (As time goes on, and more trouble codes are added, there may be letters added in place of or in addition to some of the numbers.) You can give this information to your tech, which they will verify, and then do some pinpoint testing to zero in on the faulty component or wiring. If you are the curious type, which I am by nature, you can go to www.obd-codes.com, and then click on the "Trouble Codes" tab at the top of the page. On this page you can find out what a particular code means and what caused it to set. This website has a wealth of diagnostic code information. Sometimes this site will even tell you how serious the failure is.

There are hundreds if not thousands of reasons that your vehicle may store a trouble code and your Check Engine or SES light come on. However, the following are some of the most common reasons we run across in the repair business.

P0440 to P0449: Evaporative Emissions Codes

These are codes that are generally P0440 to P0449, and many of the older vehicles on the road today have one or more of these codes stored. It can be as simple as tightening your gas cap or it can get more involved like a bad sensor a vapor leak on top of the fuel tank. These codes typically will not affect how your vehicle is running; however, in some states or localities it may be the reason that your car failed an inspection. The downside of not getting this repaired, and the code cleared, is that your check engine or Service Engine Soon light will remain lit, hiding any more serious underlying conditions. In other words, if the check engine light is already on for an evap failure, you won't know when your vehicle has a lean running condition until it starts running so poorly that you may need a tow. Therefore, although evaporative emission codes don't usually affect the drivability of your car, it's always best to get them taken care of and the codes cleared from the PCM's memory.

The top three causes for an evap code are a loose or faulty fuel cap, a vent valve or purge valve. There are many other possible but less common causes as well. If your check engine light came on a day or two after you filled up with gas, check your fuel cap and make sure that it is tight. If it was loose, it may take a day or two for the light to go off.

During the troubleshooting process, your technician may ask for your approval to "smoke test" your car's evap system. Simply put, they will introduce smoke into the closed evap system and then inspect the fittings, valves, lines, fuel cap and fuel tank for any smoke leaking out indicating where the leak is. Sometimes if the stored code is a "small leak detected" code, it may take some time to pinpoint the leak, where larger leaks are usually easier to locate.

P0562: Low System Voltage

Code P0562 indicates that the PCM has detected a low voltage condition in the electrical system. This can be a little tricky because many times this code may be stored in history: for some reason the battery was run down and then recharged, perhaps during a "no crank" condition that we discussed earlier. If your alternator has an intermittent no charge condition, this code could set.

P0128: Thermostat Below Regulated Temperature

Thermostats have been used to control the operating temperature of the engine for many years by regulating the flow of the engine coolant through the radiator. Before computerized engine control systems, the only way the driver knew that the thermostat failed was either the heater wouldn't get warm in the winter time (stuck open) or the engine would over heat (stuck closed). For the overheating condition, if everything was in the driver's favor, an engine overheating light would come on, or if you were really driving in style, you may have a gauge that would show you that the engine's temperature was above normal. Many times, by the time the overheating light came on, it was too late, and the driver would see steam rolling out from under the hood and the damage to the engine may have already been done.

Today, the power train control module monitors the engine temperature by using one or more engine and radiator coolant temperature sensors. When the PCM sees the temperature is not being regulated properly within preset parameters, or it notices that something isn't quite right with the cooling system or one of its sensors, then is will set a code like P0128 or perhaps a P0116 among others. The result is that repairs can be made before the thermostat completely fails and your engine overheats.

P0300 to P0312: Misfire Codes

These codes are biggies and the driver will usually know if it is consistent. These misfire codes start with P0300, which is a random engine misfire. In other words, the PCM has not detected a specific cylinder misfiring because the misfire is jumping around from one cylinder to another. If the trouble code ends in a number other than zero, this will indicate which cylinder is misfiring. So a trouble code P0303 indicates that cylinder number three is misfiring. Your turn now: if the trouble code is a P0307, which cylinder is misfiring? You're absolutely correct! Cylinder number seven is the one misfiring. Pretty easy huh? Sometimes you'll see a P0300 in combination with a specific cylinder code.

Now there are many things that can cause an engine to misfire, but the most common are old and worn-out spark plugs or a faulty ignition coil. Usually on higher mileage vehicles, when I question the customer, if the spark plugs have not been replaced, then that is the first step. As I mentioned earlier in the book, with platinum or iridium spark plugs going 100,000 miles before they are changed, this makes it easier to forget about them until a misfire and trouble code(s) appear.

If the vehicle is newer or the plugs have been replaced, then the misfire is most likely due to some other failure or condition. A failed or plugged fuel injector could cause a misfire, as could a dirty or faulty MAF sensor. Internal engine damage resulting in low cylinder compression could also cause an engine misfire. A compression and/or a cylinder leak down test performed by your technician can verify this. In short, there are a multitude of reasons that your car may be misfiring. The key is to get in to your technician as soon as possible before further damage is done, possibly resulting in the following.

P0420 to P0434: Catalyst Efficiency Below Threshold

Generally, these codes are due to the following: oxygen sensor failure, the efficiency of the catalytic convertor has degraded, or the catalytic convertor is restricted (plugged).

What is a catalytic convertor and what is it used for? In simple terms, the convertor (for short) is a device located in the exhaust system right after the exhaust manifold, which is attached to your vehicle's engine. The purpose of the convertor is to reduce air pollution by reducing three things in your car's exhaust: hydrocarbons (HC), carbon monoxide (CO) and oxides of nitrogen (NOx).

In most cases, the catalytic convertor will last the life of the vehicle. The key to this however is to maintain the performance of the engine. If the engine is neglected, then most likely the convertor will need to be replaced at some time. When the engine misfires, allowing unburnt fuel to enter the convertor, the catalytic convertor overheats and many times will begin to melt down internally. Other times, contaminants such as oil or coolant from an unmaintained engine will collect inside of the convertor, allowing deposits to build up and restrict it.

Although an inefficient convertor may just trigger a check engine light, with no symptoms for the driver to detect, a restricted convertor is another story. A plugged catalytic convertor will usually be obvious to the driver. At first it may be gradual, but as the problem progresses, the sensation of the vehicle not being able to get out of its own way will be present. You're sitting at a stop light when it turns green, you try to accelerate but your car just doesn't want to go without a struggle. You can hear the engine bog as you press harder on the accelerator as it slowly gets going. To simulate this, take a deep breath, now cover your mouth with your hand while pinching of your nose, and now try to exhale. It's hard, isn't it? This is why your car won't accelerate as it used to. Many times the exhaust will have an odd rotten egg smell associated with a restricted catalytic convertor.

Catalytic convertors are pretty durable and will last a long time if you take care of them. They are a necessary part of your vehicle, so when they fail, replacement is the only option. In fact, in some cities or states where automobile inspections are required, if you fail the emissions test, you fail the inspection.

Replacing catalytic convertors can get to be very expensive; usually it's in the neighborhood of $900 to $1,500 or more. This is why it is very important to get the engine's misfire condition corrected as quickly as possible. The best and most cost-effective way to keep your catalytic convertor in top condition is to keep up on all of the maintenance schedules that your vehicle's manufacturer has established for your make and model of car or truck.

P0130 to P0167: Oxygen Sensor Failures

These particular codes refer to oxygen sensor failures. On modern vehicles, oxygen sensors are located in the exhaust system before (upstream of) and after (downstream of) the catalytic convertor(s). Your technician may refer to the upstream sensor as an air/fuel sensor because it has a wider range than the downstream sensor, but perhaps some of the more technical details are better left for another time or book. For now we'll just call them both oxygen sensors because that is what they essentially do: sense how much oxygen is remaining in the exhaust.

The oxygen sensors play a very crucial part in keeping your car running at peak performance. Although the upstream and downstream both monitor the oxygen content of the exhaust, they each play a different role.

The primary mission of the upstream oxygen sensor or air/fuel sensor is to monitor the remaining oxygen content after the engine's air/fuel combustion process. If there is too much oxygen remaining in the exhaust, then the engine is running too "lean"; if there is too little, the engine is running "rich." This bit of information is then sent to your car's computer (PCM), allowing it to make the correct air fuel adjustments to keep it running at its peak efficiency.

The job of the downstream oxygen sensor is to monitor the efficiency of the catalytic convertor. Where the upstream sensor signal will be fluctuating up and down rapidly with the rapidly changing air/fuel mixture controlled by the PCM, the downstream signal will hold fairly steady, indicating that the catalytic convertor is doing its job. If your technician sees that the signal from the downstream oxygen sensor is changing rapidly along with the upstream sensor, then they will suspect a possible catalytic convertor efficiency problem, which we just covered.

Oxygen sensors can fail for a variety of reasons, but given the nature of their job, they usually wear out and become sluggish or stop working altogether. When these sensors fail, there may or may not be any obvious symptoms. The downstream sensor often times will only set a code and trigger the check engine light to come on. The upstream can cause a rough running condition or you may notice a change in your vehicle's fuel economy. Some texts may include oxygen sensors under the "tune-up" heading for obvious reasons. Because they play such a vital role in the performance and drivability of your car, I monitor the performance of the oxygen sensors when the spark plugs are replaced and recommend replacing them if they start setting diagnostic trouble codes or if the data that I see is looking a bit flaky.

Although there are many sensors before and during the combustion process of your vehicle's engine, essentially the oxygen sensors are the only post-combustion sensors. If the exhaust's oxygen content input to the PCM is skewed, it will eventually cause changes to your vehicle's engine performance.

P0100 to P0109: MAF and MAP Sensor Codes

Although I listed P0100 through P0109, the two of these codes that are probably most common are P0101 (Mass Air Flow Range/Performance Problem) and P0106 (Manifold Absolute Pressure Range/Performance Problem).

The MAF (Mass Air Flow) sensor is located somewhere between the air filter and the intake manifold. The purpose of the MAF sensor is to monitor the air flowing into the engine. The MAP (Manifold Absolute Pressure) sensor is located on the intake manifold and its job is to monitor the pressure (vacuum) inside of the intake manifold. Under various load and driving conditions, like when your car is idling at a stop or you're accelerating into traffic, these two sensors constantly relay this information to the PCM, which in turn makes fuel adjustments (fuel trim).

The symptoms of either of these sensors failing, or the MAF sensor being dirty, is a rough running and/or stalling engine. If your vehicle is un-drivable, you've scanned it for codes, and it comes up with an MAF sensor trouble code, one thing you can try is to shut off the ignition switch, and locate and unplug the MAF sensor. Before doing this, however, write down any codes that were stored before unplugging the sensor; you will want to give this list of codes to your technician. Now see if your vehicle will start and run smooth enough to get it to your repair shop. On <u>some</u> vehicles, this will allow the PCM to use a default MAF mode. Note: this is NOT a repair or a fix, and it will not work on all vehicles. It WILL set other MAF sensor codes, so when you talk to your technician, let them know that it is unplugged so that they don't look under the hood, plug the MAF back in and assume that the problem is corrected. Communication with your tech is critical. Also note: on some vehicles when you unplug the MAF sensor, the vehicle won't run at all. If this is the case, simply turn off the ignition and plug the MAF back in.

P0171 and P0174: Lean Code

These two codes P0171 and P0174 are also common. These occur when the PCM detects, via the oxygen sensors, that the engine is running in a lean condition: the sensors are detecting too much oxygen in the exhaust.

Although there are many things that can cause these two trouble codes to set, based on my experience, vacuum leaks are at the top of the list, followed by a dirty or faulty MAF sensor (remember the college student who cleaned her MAF sensor and corrected the problem?) or faulty oxygen sensors.

To operate properly, both the exhaust and intake systems need to be sealed. In other words, the exhaust only exits through the tail pipe and not through any leaks in the exhaust system, especially not in front of the catalytic convertors. Likewise, the intake system, where the air enters the engine for combustion, cannot have any air entering unless it enters through the air filtration system and through the MAF sensor. Any air that enters into the air intake system after the air filter will be considered a vacuum leak. Any unfiltered air entering the MAF sensor can potentially contaminate the sensor and set a trouble code and/or cause severe drivability problems with your engine.

Leaks that occur in the air intake system after the MAF sensor will probably set a P0171 or P0174, or possibly both at the same time, depending on the location of the leak. On an engine that has an in-line cylinder configuration, like an in-line four (I4) or six (I6), or bank 1 of an engine with a V configuration like a V6, V8, etc., a P0171 trouble code will indicate a leak that is only affecting that bank on the engine. Likewise, a P0174 trouble code will indicate a leak that is only affecting bank 2 on a V configured engine. By identifying which of the codes are set individually or together, your technician will be able to test certain areas that are prone to vacuum leaks, pinpoint and then correct the problem.

The most common symptoms for this condition are a rough or high idle, hesitation or surging while trying to accelerate, or lack of power.

There Won't Be a Test on This Later

Okay, I know that this is a lot to digest all at once. There is no need to memorize all of these codes and no, there won't be a test on them later. As I mentioned earlier, there are hundreds of diagnostic codes, but these are probably the most common of the codes that we see. In fact, they are so common that many experienced techs have most of these codes, which I just mentioned, stored away in their memory banks! If you have a little knowledge of what they are, you'll be miles ahead when it comes to talking to your technician. The thing that I would like for you to take away from this section is not to ignore what your car or truck is telling you. If the "Check Engine" or "Service Engine Soon" light comes on, get it checked out; if not, eventually it will end up costing you more either in the repair shop or at the gas pump.

In addition, once your tech makes any necessary repairs, ask them to clear any of the codes that were stored. If they do not, then this could throw another tech off if there is the need to rescan the PCM for another condition or problem. At some point, the PCM is smart enough to know and clear the code, if after a certain amount of ignition or drive cycles there is no longer a problem present. It may still be present in the history data, however. I just find that it is a good practice to remember that no repair is complete until the trouble code has been cleared from the PCM's memory.

What Diagnostic Trouble Codes Are and What They Aren't

Diagnostic trouble codes *ARE* a helpful tool or guide, but that's all they are and nothing more. They *ARE NOT* intended to be a diagnosis. Too often some discount auto parts store is all too eager to come out, read a diagnostic code and then sell you a part. If that doesn't work then they will sell you another part, and another and so on. I like to call this Easter egging: the problem isn't diagnosed, but one part after another is replaced in the hope that one of those parts will be the lucky part that fixes your car.

About three years ago I had a new customer get his truck towed to my shop after he had installed a fuel pump to correct a low fuel pressure condition. While the vehicle was still able to start and run, the man took it to an auto parts store to have the codes read. Eventually the auto parts employee sold him a fuel pump which my customer promptly installed (not a fun job), only to still have the same problem that eventually got worse to the point that is wouldn't start or run at all.

After doing an initial scan, I found trouble codes P0171 and P0174 stored among others relating to the ignition system. I tested the fuel and ignition systems to find that they were not within the factory specification. After checking the voltage going to the fuel pump module, I discovered that there was only a little over 8 volts present when there should have been close to 12.6 volts, battery voltage. Long story short, and without going through all of the diagnostic steps taken, the root cause was a failure in the ignition switch circuit, not the fuel pump. A new ignition switch and he was on his way.

The moral of the story is, although diagnostic trouble codes can be interesting and helpful in the diagnostic process, if not followed up with proper testing by your technician, they can send you out in left field. The customer of mine didn't really save any money in this case because the proper diagnosis wasn't made at the parts store. Auto parts stores sell parts and that's it, they don't diagnose. Other than a few quick things you can check, its best to let your technician diagnose the root cause of the problem, especially if the repair is time consuming or the parts are costly, which on today's vehicles is quite common. In the end, I gained a very happy customer!

The No-code Condition

We've just covered some of the most common causes for the "Check Engine" or "Service Engine Soon" light to illuminate on your instrument cluster or driver information center. As I mentioned, there are hundreds of diagnostic codes and virtually thousands of scenarios that could cause those codes to set and the light to come on.

Although the control modules have become very advanced, they aren't perfect or a replacement for your technician. Sometimes a vehicle will roll into the shop having an electrical issue or will intermittently die without warning. A complete system scan shows no trouble codes present. This is known as a "no-code condition." What this means is that the problem is so sporadic that the control modules have not yet detected the problem. Or, it's so rare that there are no codes that have been engineered or associated with that problem. In these cases, a technician has to roll up his or her sleeves and dig in, using their past experiences, the experiences of others and wade through dozens of pages of service manuals and technical service bulletins. It may take some time, but if you have a trustworthy tech, they will get to the root of the problem. You'll need to be patient, however. Not every problem is cut and dried, and there is a diagnostic process that most technicians are taught to go through on their way to repairing your vehicle.

A Word About Reprogramming (Re-flashing)

Most of us are quite familiar with the laptops, tablets, smart phones, and the need for software updates. However, did you know that your car requires software updates as well? Yes, from time to time automobile manufacturers will come out with a new software update for any one of the many control modules that your vehicle has on board. Most of the time you won't even know about these software updates unless there is a safety recall involving one.

More often, there may be a technical service bulletin covering a particular problem with the vehicle. For example, we had a vehicle that came in with the check engine light on and a stored code indicating that there was a problem with one of the oxygen sensors. There were no drivability concerns. After test driving the vehicle, the data looked fine on both the upstream oxygen sensor and the downstream oxygen sensor. So we cleared the code and sent the customer on their way and told them to return if the light came back on.

A few days later the customer returned with the same code present. After digging a little deeper we found that the factory parameters were too narrow and that there was a re-flash to correct the problem. After re-flashing the PCM with updated software, those narrow parameters were opened up a little and the issue was resolved. This was not an isolated incident. After replacing the battery on one customer's car, the battery light was staying on even though the battery was fully charged and the alternator was charging. It took a re-flash or a reprogramming of the power train control module to correct this issue as well.

Sometimes there may not be any outward issues, but with a simple reprogramming of a control module, that system may work more efficiently. On the other hand, many electrical or drivability problems have been corrected with a simple re-flash, no parts needed. Check with your local dealership to see if there are any updates available for your vehicle. For a small fee they will check and update any control modules that have updated software available. I would however advise that you stick with your dealership for this service, unless your tech at the shop that you use is familiar with the reprogramming procedures for your make and model of car. Under normal circumstances re-flashing a vehicle will usually take about thirty minutes or less to complete at the dealership.

Are You Your Car's Best Friend or Worst Enemy?

Most drivers, from the first time that they get behind the wheel, pamper and take good care of their set of wheels. Their car is their livelihood, getting them back and forth to work, to their family reunion or to pick up that hot date that they were dreaming about throughout high school. Yeah, I remember what is was like, to wash and vacuum out the car just before I picked up my movie and dinner date (grin)... Oh wait! Back to the book—sorry about that, I drifted off for a moment... Anyway, there are a few (and you know who you are) who may not quite yet appreciate how durable yet delicate our cars and trucks are to the extremes of nature that can be avoided all together. Forget about the commercials you see on TV about how durable or tough their cars or trucks are, in the end they won't hold up if they aren't taken care of.

Okay, as harsh as this may sound, I'll get right to the point. There are some drivers who are their car's worst enemy. Yeah, I said it, and here's why. Here are probably the top two problems that are driver induced or preventable. I stand corrected: top on the list is lack of regular maintenance, including oil changes. I've already talked about the importance of this, so I don't want to beat the importance of regular maintenance to death. But the facts are clear: this is the number one reason vehicles die a premature death. Now onto the other: owner or operator preventable damages to their vehicles.

Rodents Belong Out in the Wild, not Under Your Hood

Next on that list would be rodent damage. Damage caused by mice, chipmunks, squirrels and even woodchucks (ground hogs) can be severe. And yes, this is a very common problem. Almost weekly we see rodent damaged vehicles get towed to the shop for repairs.

The most common things that many shops see are rodent nests built inside the air cleaner or in the blower motor housing and chewed wiring harnesses. This is not something that is just a country living problem; it happens in the city as well. Many times the little critters will build nests or store food inside of your vehicle somewhere causing your engine to suffocate and stop running, as in the illustration (page 122). They will also jam up your blower motor preventing you from using your air conditioner or heater.

The damage that can be done to your car's wiring can be extensive if left unchecked and the rodents aren't eradicated from the premises or your car isn't protected in some way. This is where the "driver prevented" statement comes from. Where you park your vehicle will make it more or less susceptible to this kind of damage.

Walnuts stored in an intake hose.

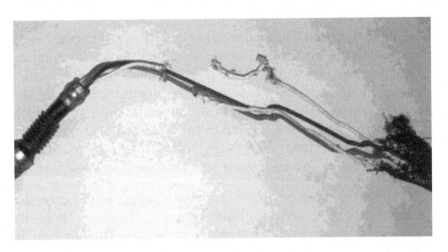

Wiring that was damaged by a rodent.

If you have a garage, this is the best place for your vehicle as long as you don't store any food or sources of nesting for the rodents in there as well. Bird seed, pet food, straw, etc. are things that will attract the rodents to your garage. If you must keep these items in the garage, keep them in an airtight tote or container where mice can't get in. If you have a rodent infestation problem, it may be a good idea to employ a pest eradication service to help. Also, talk to your technician: sometimes simply putting rodent baits under the hood and around your car will help keep the little buggers from making your car or truck their next place of residence. Your tech will tell you where the best place is to put the baits under the hood, or they can do it for you. It is important not to put it around any moving engine components or where is will interfere with the operation of your car.

It's Not a Speed Boat

Another example of a "driver induced" car problem is driving through floodwaters. Yup, this happens every time there are heavy rains and where streets or roadways become flooded. A driver who is in a hurry or just doesn't want to find an alternate route will attempt to drive through the high waters. They get just far enough for the water to be sucked up into the air intake and kill the engine (sometimes literally). At best you'll be calling a tow truck and spend a few hundred dollars cleaning the water out of the air filter box and intake manifold. At worst, the engine will hydro lock. This is when the cylinders of the engine become filled with water, and we all know that water does not compress like air does. The end result is probable major engine damage costing thousands of dollars.

As a side note—and no this isn't scientific—my surmise after questioning several customers is that there may be a direct correlation between the speed of the water's entry and the price of the repairs. Therefore, I would not recommend putting this theory to the test; just remember that your car is not a speed boat.

The engine damage just mentioned is not all, however. Another thing to consider is that many times the water will invade electrical connections, leaving your car susceptible to years of electrical issues and repairs. Moreover, that's still not all: if water gets inside of the passenger compartment, the carpet padding or possibly the whole carpet may need to be replaced. Simply put, if you see water flooding the roadway, stop and turn around, don't try to go through it. Those few seconds or minutes may cost you or save you thousands of dollars.

Although those were probably the top two, in terms of frequency and costliness, of driver preventable problems, the list doesn't stop there. Here are some more matters that are driver induced that are completely avoidable that shops run across.

Small Keepsakes, Big Problems

Okay, this may seem quite strange to many of you, but this little point that I'm about to make will help you from getting stranded somewhere because you weren't able to start your car. Here is the scenario: you insert your key into the ignition and it starts to catch and not turn. It takes a couple of times before you are able to turn the key, which allows the engine to start cranking over and start. At first it's a rare thing, and then it becomes more frequent until it gets to the point where if left uncorrected, it will eventually leave you stranded. Sometimes you can't get the key out of the ignition, other times the ignition switch just won't turn.

The cause for this is worn tumblers within the ignition lock cylinder itself. Under normal conditions, these lock cylinders will last for years without causing any problems. However, we have seen this condition hastened by the driver by adding excessive items to the keychain, creating an excessive load on the ignition tumblers. To avoid this, only put what is necessary on your key chain and no more. A good rule of thumb is, if your key ring feels heavy when you hold it in your hand, then it's probably too heavy.

This will cause premature lock cylinder failure

Although souvenirs are a great way to remember that trip that you took to Madagascar last summer, or those charms remind you of that special life changing event, that extra weight on your car's key ring will spell certain premature destruction to the ignition lock cylinder, costing you several hundred dollars for your tech or lock smith to repair. The good news is that many car manufacturers are moving toward a push button ignition system, eliminating the need for the lock cylinder altogether.

Pop, Soda, Coke...

Years ago, you generally had a couple of options when it came to shifting your automatic transmission into gear. Either you had a gear shift lever on the steering column, or on some models you had push buttons on the dash. These were fairly simple mechanisms with little to no safety precautions engineered into them. As time progressed into the sixties and seventies, the more sporty automatic shift lever on the floor with bucket seats came into vogue. Along with those floor shifters, eventually safety devices were engineered into them, keeping the vehicle from accidently being shifted out of "Park" by an innocent child just, well...being a child.

You may be thinking: "Enough with the history lesson, get on with it already." Okay: Pop, Soda, Coke, or whatever you may call it in the part of the country that you are from, these sticky beverages of choice have been the demise of many a floor shifting mechanism. Spilled onto, and eventually into the gear shifter assemblies, shifting out of park will eventually become nearly impossible.

Tucked away deep inside of that sporty shifter console, mounted onto the shifter assembly itself, is a little electrical solenoid called a shift interlock solenoid. Its one and only purpose in life is to keep anyone from shifting the vehicle out of "Park," unless the driver turns the ignition on and depresses the brake pedal. This is that engineering marvel that keeps a vehicle from rolling around and into the street, when junior wants to see what happens when he pulls on that stick or lever.

When syrupy liquids get spilled onto the mechanism or onto the shift interlock solenoid, it can't do its job. Here is the symptom that you'll eventually experience: you get into your car, put your foot on the brake, and start it. Next, you attempt to shift it into "Reverse" or "Drive," but you can't. The shifter won't budge. Again, you just created another repair bill that your tech will love you for. So how do you prevent this from happening? Keep any liquids away from the dash or shifter assembly.

To help avoid a tow bill, many vehicles have a manual interlock release so that the driver can shift it into gear. It is usually not very easy to get to, else the shifter interlock system would be rather pointless. If you have this no shift condition, contact your technician and they may be able to instruct you on how to manually get your car into gear and get it into the shop for repairs. Do not do this unless you are instructed to by your tech. It's better to call a tow truck than to cause more damage to your vehicle.

Secure That Cargo!

I want to end this chapter with a helpful pointer I learned from experience. It doesn't matter if you're driving a car or truck, if you are carrying cargo or fluids in a container, tie it down, strap it up or secure it in some way to keep it from shifting when you apply the brakes.

Recently a young woman asked me how to get a smell of gasoline out of her car. I asked how she had got the gasoline smell in her car to begin with. She said she had bought some gas in a container and then put the container on the back seat unsecured. She had to make an emergency stop, the can fell forward and the cap came off, spilling gasoline all over her carpet.

When hauling heavy items or liquids like gasoline, put the items in the trunk (or in the back cargo area, if you're driving an SUV). First lay an old blanket or sheet down and then place the items as far forward as possible in that compartment. This way, if you have to make an emergency stop, the items can't slide or tip forward. Wedge them in with rags or other items like boxes. (Don't keep gasoline in your vehicle for very long as the vapors are hazardous and bad for your health.) With lots of kitty litter, carpet cleaning and fresh air, the smell in the young woman's car is mostly gone.

Chapter 6: Choosing a Repair Shop and Technician, What to Look For

I've been asked this question a lot over the years: "How do I find a good reliable repair shop or mechanic?" This is probably one of the hardest questions to answer because understanding the people you associate with on a daily basis can be tricky and it is no different when it comes to finding a trusted repair shop or technician. Sometimes it may take a few visits to different shops to find that one shop that you can trust completely to give you accurate analysis of your vehicle's condition. But when you do find that one shop or that one tech, it'll be a relationship that will last for years, just like your doctor, dentist or CPA. Many just call whatever shop can get them in right away or is the least expensive, but is that the best way to approach it? Let's find out.

When I started up my repair business I went to SCORE (Service Core of Retired Executives) for guidance. They counseled me on many things and gave me a lot of sound advice. The one thing that stuck out, however, was when they advised me to pick out one or two things to do and be really good at doing them—the best! Don't try to be all things to all people; I would just end up being mediocre and very frustrated. They also said that when I'd established myself as one of the best among my peers, word would get out around town.

There are many excellent shops out there, working hard to be the best among their competitors. In addition, unfortunately there are many shops that are poor as well. Then there are those that are just mediocre, just getting by. The good shops out there aren't going to be the cheapest. Unfortunately, that's a fact of life. Have you ever heard the saying, "You get what you pay for"? This is especially true with auto repair shops. You want someone to do a cheap job? Then you'll get... well, a cheap job. The best shops will generally demand higher labor rates; this is required to maintain the best technicians and support team on staff. Also, they will use quality parts, which again won't be the least expensive.

Where to Look

If you don't already have a reputable repair shop, here are a few places you can start looking.

Personal Reference: At the top of the list is personal references or recommendations. You won't go wrong with good referrals; especially several good referrals to the same shop. I'm sure you've heard it said, "Bad news travels fast." The news of a business with a bad reputation will travel much faster than its counterpart with a good rep. In any case, the first place to go to find a good shop is to their other satisfied customers. This may be a good friend of yours or a cousin or parent.

The best advertisement is word of mouth; hands down, the most successful businesses rely heavily on this. Its free advertising and nothing beats a good testimonial. So before you decide to "Easter egg" for a repair shop or tech, go right to the people you know and trust. They'll tell you straight up where to find good shops as well as the establishments to shy away from. The best referrals come from those who have had a long-standing relationship with their repair facility.

Here are some questions to ask: Overall, are you satisfied with your shop? Are they skilled? In other words, over the years have they generally repaired a vehicle the first time or are they parts replacers? Do they back up their work with some sort of warranty? Are they reliable? If they say that a car will be done by Thursday, will it be? On the other hand, are the vehicles habitually completed a week or two after the date promised? Some shops like to over-promise and under-deliver, getting the vehicles in and backlogged, not worrying about when they can get to it.

Don't worry about the dollars and cents. Yes, that's what I said; at this point don't put a lot of weight on the cost of the repairs. You're looking for a GOOD shop, and generally, repair costs among reputable shops are going to be fairly consistent. If a shop comes back with a quote that is significantly lower, buyer beware. Make sure you're comparing apples to apples: look at the parts and labor breakdown of each quote. The point here is that professionalism, quality and reliability are worth their weight in gold—and certainly worth the few extra dollars that you may have to pay to get that kind of service.

Recently I quoted a job to a customer; it included replacing the power steering gear and hoses that were leaking. The customer thought we were a little too high on our quote, so trading in our thirty-five plus years of experience went to a big chain repair facility where they undercut our prices. They did the job; however, the customer had to return to that shop three times because the job wasn't done correctly and kept leaking large quantities of power steering fluid. Giving up on them, they brought their vehicle back to us. We found that the hose had been cross-threaded into the steering gear, not allowing it to seal properly. Because the fitting was cross-threaded into the steering gear, both the hose and steering gear had been damaged. To correct this, the steering gear would need to be replaced again, along with the hose. We took pictures and recommended that the customer take the vehicle along with the pictures back a fourth time and apply more pressure to the shop that did the original inferior work. For us to fix the problem, the customer would have been charged again for what should have been done correctly the very first time. That customer was sent on their way three times! This is basic stuff, the car should never have left the other shop in this condition. This is why I say, price goes to the bottom of the list of criteria for finding a great shop.

If you're motivated only by getting the cheapest repairs possible, it's time for you to put this book down and head on over to Sleazy Eddy's down the street, whose mission statement reads, "We'll beat 'em and cheat 'em." Of course, I say this tongue in cheek, but there are shops out there that, although they may not outwardly proclaim such a notion, it is self-evident by the lack of quality put into their shops and repairs. These are the shops whose mission is to bring in more work by being the cheapest shop in town, not the best. If they never see you again, not to worry: it's on to the next gullible customer that falls for the cheapest job in town ploy. Perhaps you've also heard the phrase associated with P.T Barnum, "There's a sucker born every minute"? Don't be that sucker.

ASE certification: Certification by the National Institute for Automotive Service Excellence (www.ase.com) is another great way to help find a good shop. A shop that voluntarily becomes ASE certified shows that they are putting forth the effort that I mentioned earlier to better themselves and stay on top of the changes that are never ending. As with so much in life, this is no guarantee, so probe deeper.

Don't let the ASE sign out front or in the lobby fool you, ask to see their credentials. Somewhere hanging on the wall in the office or shop there should be the certificates of all of the technicians who are certified and all of the technical areas they are certified in. Take time to look at them. How many certificates are on the wall? Now how many techs are employed there, or working in the shop? Believe it or not, some shops may employ one or two techs that are certified, the shop is ASE certified, and yet there may be seven guys doing work on vehicles for which they aren't certified. Some say, "Well ASE certification doesn't mean anything," or "You don't have to be certified to be good." This is true. Nevertheless, when you're looking for a technician to work on your car or truck, do you want to take that chance? You don't have to be certified to be an accountant, but I won't take my taxes to one who isn't a CPA.

ASA Member: The Automotive Service Association (www.asashop.org) is a good place to search for a shop as well. Member shops who voluntarily join ASA strive for perfection in training and customer services. Here is what they say in their own words:

> "The Automotive Service Association (ASA) advances professionalism and excellence in the automotive repair industry through education, representation and member services. Since 1951, the Automotive Service Association (ASA) has been the leading organization for owners and managers of automotive service businesses that strive to deliver excellence in service and repairs to consumers."

So check out their website www.asashop.org. There you can search for member shops in your area.

BBB: Of course, everybody has heard of the Better Business Bureau. Go to www.bbb.org to investigate a shop in our area. You can check out their ratings: any shop with an "A" rating is probably a safe bet. One can find any outstanding complaints filed against that shop as well as any of the shops rebuttals. Do not discount any shop due to a single complaint filed. A shop can't please 100% of its customers 100% of the time, and there will always be that one consumer that will never be completely pleased, no matter what the shop owner does or gives them. Enough about that however, perhaps that is a subject for another book or blog. At www.bbb.org, you will also find information about the company like the owner's name, how long they've been in business and any other pertinent information. This is another good resource to help narrow your search for a good repair facility.

You've Found Your Auto Repair Shop, Now What?

Okay you've done your homework online or gotten some good personal recommendations and you think you've found a shop. Here are a few questions to ask them that will help you quickly weed out the mediocre shops from the top-notch ones.

Identifix or iATN

Ask the shop service writer or tech if they subscribe to Identifix or iATN. If they give you a puzzled look, then run away and keep looking. If the shop representative says "No," then you may also want to move on to the next repair shop, and here's why.

Identifix and iATN are sister websites that are available to help technicians diagnose difficult problems. In simple terms, Identifix is a tech support site where a tech can call and speak to a professional with years of experience dedicated to a specific make of vehicle. iATN is another fee based site that shops can subscribe to that offers input and advice from techs around the world to help with certain hard to diagnose problems.

Although techs can be well trained and constantly stay up to date with the latest changes, no one can have the answer to all of the problems that may arise in the modern automobile. Dealerships have had tech support systems in place for years; the independent shops have Identifix. So, it's a big world out there if a shop decides to go it alone. You get a vehicle that has a certain intermittent symptom with no diagnostic codes, where do you go for help? With a smaller shop, if none of the other techs have seen that problem before, they can very well find themselves lost, perhaps guessing and charging you for that guess. Remember the parts replacer I told you about earlier? With Identifix or iATN, a tech has the whole world at their disposal, and thousands of accumulated years of experience. In turn, they can get to the correct area and the root cause without wasting precious time and charging you for it.

Here is a case in point. A 2004 Chrysler Sebring comes into the shop for the following condition. At a stop light, intermittently the speedometer will read 15 miles per hour while the car is sitting still. Also, randomly the transmission will shift from first gear to second, again while sitting still. This may happen twice a day or go for a week without it happening. No diagnostic codes, where do you start looking? In the transmission? The instrument cluster? Remember, this only happens intermittently, so trying to find it using pinpoint testing is pointless. After going to Identifix, we found several other techs had run across the same problem and corrected it with an alternator replacement. So after doing one simple recommended test that took approximately 20 seconds, while the vehicle briefly acted up in the shop, we knew that the problem lay in the alternator. We quoted and replaced the alternator and the customer went away happy, never to have the symptoms return.

So if you want a shop that has the diagnostic power of thousands of techs and the help of a tech support team, find one that subscribes to one or both of these services. You'll be glad that you did!

Ask to See the Shop

A clean shop is an organized and efficient shop. Likewise, a messy shop is a recipe for chaos and disaster. On your first visit to a shop, try to get a peek into the shop to see the work conditions there. Image is everything: if the shop is sloppy and the techs unkempt, then why would they treat your car, your pride and joy, any different?

Most shops that have procedures in place for checking in your car, shop clean up and dress codes for their employees, will take the same pride in your vehicle as they do for their work environment. I've personally seen vehicles sustain substantial damage because the shop was cluttered up with so much junk that the vehicle had to be squeezed into the repair bay; thus, any wrong move and the paint could have been scratched or the fender dented. What about seat covers and floor mats? Any shop working on your vehicle should install these covers to prevent a tech from getting dirt or grease on the inside of your vehicle. The tech that just did an oil change or replaced transmission cooler lines (a messy job) will probably be the one sitting in the driver's seat and test driving your vehicle.

Hire a Technician, Not a Mechanic

Throughout this book you've heard me use the term "technician" rather than mechanic to describe today's automotive professional. Here's why.

Although this may sound harsh or may even be offensive to some, this is the reasoning behind my statement. Years ago, auto repair professionals were called mechanics. Their toolboxes usually contained a few sets of wrenches, fixed and adjustable, assorted socket sets and some hammers. As time goes on, however, the title "mechanic" is becoming a dying term. Yes, those who refuse to keep up or invest in the future of automotive repair will still be considered mechanics, but as everything goes electronic, this won't be the case for much longer.

Today's professionals require much larger toolboxes that contain much more than wrenches and hammers. They may have a couple of scan tools, a lab scope, leak down testers, specialty tools for working on certain engines. Several types of pullers, crimpers, infrared testers, testers for measuring temperature and backpressure, bore scopes and multi-meters. Leak detectors, electronic ears, and the list goes on. When a new model car or truck becomes available for sale to the public there will usually be some specialty tool that will be required to repair it.

Most of the scanners that are found in the shop are very high tech and can get to be very expensive, starting out at about $1,500 and going up from there. Along with the scanners, scopes and multimeters, most technicians have several thousand dollars invested in their tool inventory. The low end would be approximately $10,000 to $20,000 for a technician starting out. A more experienced tech will have well over $30,000 invested in tools and equipment.

Today's serious techs are constantly receiving updated training through classes or clinics in the evening after work or through online sources. This training isn't free: either they pay for it or their employer pays for it. Another way to think about it is this: Your physician pretty much works on the same body that's been around for millennia, in which nothing has changed except perhaps treatment practices. Your tech has to stay on top of all of the changes that are coming down the pipe on a yearly basis. Just when they got used to replacing the battery that was under the hood, engineers move it to the trunk, or under the rear seat or tucked away inside the front fender. Light bulbs that used to take five minutes to change may now take an hour or two to replace. The turbo charged four-cylinder dual cam variable valve timing (VVT) engine is very different to the V8 engines of the past and requires far more education and expertise to maintain or repair.

Therefore, as you can see, many of these men and women have invested enough time, money and effort in their careers to have earned the title of technician; to be the best and stand out from the rest! These are the individuals you want to seek out to work on your vehicle; the best of the best. The reputation of the auto repair shop is usually linked to the techs who work there. Bad techs or mechanics, and the shop's reputation will be bad. After all, if the cars and trucks are not repaired correctly and in a timely manner, how can the shop have a good reputation? So first, by looking for a shop with a good reputation, you will generally find a good tech there.

Can't We All Just Get Along?

Over many years of working in the customer service industry I've seen great working relationships built, and on the other hand I've witnessed service provider and customer relationships that turned into train wrecks. Here are some tips on how to have a great, long-term working relationship with your technician. Don't laugh. Think about it: what is the single most expensive thing to maintain in today's busy world outside of the home that we live in? Yup, it's that thing sitting in your driveway or garage.

Over the life of our vehicles, we will have spent thousands of dollars maintaining it. We don't bat an eyelid when it comes to spending money on a round of golf or at the hair salon, yet we moan and complain when it comes to taking our car in to be serviced or repaired. Why do most of us go to the same dentist or hair stylist for years? Is it because we trust them to make the best decisions while working on our teeth or our hair? Having a great relationship with your tech is no different and will potentially ease the blow of an unexpected repair that needs to be done. Moreover, give your tech the same courtesy as the other professionals in your life. If a client gets a bad haircut or color from their stylist, do they jump ship immediately and start looking for another stylist? Not usually, unless bad haircuts become a trend.

That said, not all personalities mesh. It is common to have a shop with two or more excellent techs working there yet some work better with certain customers than others. A particular customer may like technician A over tech B, or that other customer may like tech B over tech A. The main thing is, are you comfortable with YOUR technician? If not, try working with another. As I mentioned before, you are working toward a long-term relationship that could save you or cost you thousands of dollars.

This is how this relationship works: If you are a great customer, you pay your bills on time and stay pleasant when conversing with your tech, often times they will throw you some freebies and not even mention them on your work order, or if they do write it up will "no charge" it. However, if you like to argue with them or complain about the cost of repairs, most assuredly you won't get the freebies and you may even have the "Pain and suffering tax" added to your labor charges, not in the form of an actual tax but rather in a bumped-up labor charge. If a job calls for 1.2 hours' labor, they may add two or three tenths of an hour to your labor for keeping them on the phone for no reason other than to complain. Most people understand that there are certain professionals you work with regularly who you don't want to become argumentative with: your physician and your CPA. I'm going to add one more: your technician.

Your technician is there to help you and make a living; it does them no good to treat you poorly. So in return, treat them with the same courtesy. It's not easy for them to pick up a phone knowing that they soon may be ruining your day with the prognosis of your beloved Veronica, which you've been driving for fifteen years. As the old saying goes, don't shoot the messenger. If you do your best to remain calm or pleasant, many times word gets around the shop that you're an A1 customer and they may take some diagnostic time off of your bill or perform a couple of extra services like cleaning the throttle body or topping off your fluids for free. These little services can add up to hundreds or even thousands of dollars over the course of your relationship with them and all it takes is a pleasant smile, a "good morning" or a "I understand, after all it is an old car." I've been in some shops where the techs will vie for the privilege of working on a particular customer's vehicle. On the flip side, there are some arguments over who gets stuck with another customer's car or truck. Some techs would rather have a root canal done than have to deal with a difficult customer. Now do you want a happy or frustrated tech working on your car? If you're unsure, think about the happy or frustrated surgeon working on you. Yup, the happy tech wins every time!

On a side note, if the tech or service writer treats you poorly or disrespectfully, then run! Remember, they are working for you, not the other way around. You are GIVING them the OPPORTUNITY to work on YOUR vehicle. This relationship is a two-way street: if you don't like the way your physician treats you, then you find another one. Do the same with a repair shop. If they continue to treat people poorly, their reputation will be the instrument that will drive them out of business eventually.

A word about large repair facilities or dealerships; these shops may have many service writers and several technicians. So if you like a particular tech servicing your vehicle and you have a good working relationship with them, make sure that you speak up and let them know that you would like Cheryl or Mike working on your vehicle. If you keep quiet and don't say anything then your car will most likely be put into the repair rotation, and whoever is available when your repair order comes up will work on your car. I personally advocate trying to stick with the same one or two technicians to work on your car.

If Your Tech is Great, Throw Them a Bone

I once had a couple of customers that would only come to my shop to receive the cheap oil changes and any specials that I ran. They would ask us to fix their sagging exhaust or re-attach a splashguard free of charge while we were doing their oil change. Whenever they were given a quote for repairs, they would promptly go over to another shop to have it done with cheaper parts. Though this may seem to be honest enough on the surface, here is the problem with playing musical repair shops.

The shop that is more expensive usually has the better diagnostic equipment, tools, better parts and probably more experienced techs; as I alluded to before, there's a reason why they aren't as cheap as the other guy. When a customer pays the $100 diagnostic fee and then takes their vehicle to another shop for repairs, they tend to get pushed to the bottom of the priority list when they come back for more diagnostic work.

I eventually "fired" that customer that I was telling you about, who only came in for the oil changes and the freebies. There's a rule of thumb that I was advised to stick to by a very wise business man. He said "90% of your customers demand 10% of your time and 10% of your customers will demand 90% of your time. Fire the 10%." Now this absolutely does not mean that a paying customer who genuinely needs some extra time should be kicked to the curb—quite the opposite, they are among the first 90%. I'm referring to those who habitually take up an excessive amount of time and never purchase anything. They use the system.

Parents of College Students, Listen Up!

This little section is for those parents who are about to send their son or daughter off to college or perhaps a tech school. Having serviced vehicles of college students, I find it ironic that a parent can send their daughter off to school, perhaps hundreds of miles away, in an old car to basically fend for themselves.

Attending a college or university is supposed to be an amazing time for your young student, providing skills and memories that will help them succeed throughout their lives; make sure they're properly prepped for the adventure. Too often, the tuition is paid, and money for living expenses provided through loans or the parents. Many students fill their off time with part time jobs to help supplement the financial gaps, so everything has been taken care of, right? Wrong! What about their vehicle? Has that been properly prepared for the next four years? Often a young student's car is towed to any given repair shop and the student is ill prepared for what comes next.

Here is what you parents can do to help relieve some of the stress of a vehicle breakdown while the kids are away at school—remember, they'll have enough to concentrate on for the next few years. After you get junior or your little girl set up on campus, remember the tips I've just mentioned to you to help find them a good reliable repair shop. Also, talk to the school that they are attending: many times they may be able to recommend a trustworthy shop in the area. If your child is driving an older vehicle, as the financially responsible one, chances are you'll be talking to the shop, perhaps several states away, to get estimates, give approvals and pay the repair bill. Having that working relationship established before you leave them to go back home will help in the transition process. Remember, they just moved away from home; they may be lonely or scared, so the last thing they need is to have to deal with an unfamiliar repair shop and strangers. You might as well send them to a foreign country not being able to speak the language.

Here is another point: by getting them set up with a repair shop, you as the parent or guardian will be more at ease as well. At times, it's tough enough talking to local shops, but when you are putting your trust in a business that you will be paying potentially several hundred dollars at a time, it would be wise to know to whom you are sending your money. Who are they? In addition, what did they just do to your student's car? Trust is everything. Find out who they are and then when you pay the repair bill you can pay with the confidence that you were as diligent in that aspect of your young student's college career as with the rest.

Now, Let's Get Your Car Repaired

I've just walked you through the process of finding a reliable repair shop that you can trust. Now, in the final chapter, let's go through the estimating process, approval, repair and then picking up your vehicle. It can be confusing at times but most of the confusion stems from one shortfall, miscommunication. Many times customers are in a hurry to get to work or get home and just want to drop off their keys and take off. This is perhaps the most important few moments of getting your car or truck repaired. Communication is everything, so don't be in too big of a hurry. Dedicate a few moments to talk to the service writer, ask questions and ensure you completely understand what he or she is telling you. Again, these few moments could potentially save you hundreds or even thousands of dollars. Once you sign your name to an estimate or work order, you are giving the repair shop authorization to complete repairs, so know what you are signing!

Chapter 7: Getting Your Vehicle Repaired – What Should You Expect?

To some the auto repair business may seem like a mystical place where cars and trucks are taken and dropped off to be renewed and given a new lease on life. Of course, this day spa for these four-wheeled creatures should be free of charge, right, or at least not any more expensive than what the vehicle owner would expect? This would probably be true in a perfect world, but unfortunately at this present time, we don't live in such a world. Like a furnace or plumbing repair, there are costs associated with it. Understanding what goes into an estimate and the repair will allow you to be more at ease when you take your car in for repairs.

First, the "Write Up"

Although this may sound like a no-brainer, it truly isn't. This is the initial step that is taken to get your car or truck on the road to recovery; and yet it is one of the most fouled up areas by shops and customers alike. Before the estimate or repair order is completed, the initial information about you and your car is critical, especially if you are filling out an "after hours" sheet or envelope. Be complete with your information, full name, full address, and full phone number including area code (remember this is the age of cell phones where the number could be from anywhere). If the service writer is writing you up, then they will most likely ask you for all of this. However, if you are dropping your vehicle off after your shop has closed for the day, using the shop's "after hours" form, be complete and make sure you sign the work authorization. Many repairs are held up due to inaccurate or insufficient contact information or missing work authorization signature.

The next aspect is perhaps the best reason to drop your car off during regular business hours and is one of the most important moments. Before leaving the parking lot, do a quick "walk around," or inspection with the service writer. They should note any damage to the outside of your vehicle, any scratches, dings or broken lights or mirrors, etc. This is an important step to protect you and the shop. Now it's time for the estimate.

The Estimate

The estimate or quote is a written agreement that your technician or service writer will give you for approval before repairs can begin. When you sign this piece of paper or approve it electronically, you two are making an agreement, a contract. He or she is committing to a repair or to diagnose a problem for a specific fee, and if there are other additional associated costs they will contact you with an updated estimate for you to either approve or decline. In addition, with this contract, you agree to pay the amount you approved. If an invoice isn't paid, then most likely the repair shop will not release a customer's vehicle to them, and after a certain period with no payment a "mechanic's lien" may be placed on their vehicle.

Always remember, when you drop your car off, this initial estimate may be just a starting point. Most of the time, for a cut and dried repair, it shouldn't waver from that original estimate that you signed. For example, replacing brake parts, shocks, or struts, for the most part it's a cut and dried estimate.

Here is where the waters get a little muddy. Let's say your car's left headlight is not working and Uncle George says you need to go to the shop and get the bulb replaced. So initially, you bring it in and the service writer may have you sign an estimate for the price of the headlight bulb and the labor to install it. In addition, let's say the bulb is $24.99 and the labor is $19.95. Along with that, you'll have shop supplies and, depending on where you live, possibly sales tax added in. So we'll say that the total estimate is about $49.00. This is just to replace the headlight bulb; however, upon completion of the work the left headlight still isn't working. This is when your tech has a decision to make. They completed the work you asked them to do without any diagnosis. Does he or she ship the car without a working headlight? After all they completed their end of the contract, they replaced the bulb. Or, do they or the service writer call you with an updated estimate that involves diagnosis time and potentially further repair costs?

This is where lack of initial questions and miscommunication come into play. Some customers will get angry at the tech or service writer and complain, "You mean, I just paid you $49 and my headlight still doesn't work?!" To correct the headlight issue it potentially could go well over the initial estimate. Don't expect more than what you are asking for. To help prevent this type of miscommunication from happening, instead of asking to replace the headlight bulb, you can say, "My left headlight is not working. My Uncle George thinks it may just be a headlight bulb that is burnt out. But before you install a new bulb can you diagnose the problem first?" With that approach, there may be a diagnosis fee that you'll need to agree to pay, if it's not the bulb. However, if they get into it and find out that it was just the bulb, then most likely they won't charge you the diagnostic fee, just the cost of replacing the bulb. The difference in approaches is that the second one puts the diagnosis squarely on the shoulders of the tech, not on Uncle George.

Something for Nothing

We once had a customer come in for a two-wheel alignment. He agreed to pay $59.00, which included a test drive, suspension inspection and the alignment (you can't align a vehicle with worn or loose suspension parts). We explained all of this to the individual, including the part that if we were not able to complete the alignment due to worn parts, there would be a suspension inspection charge of $39.00. Upon inspection, we found that the lower ball joints were worn and loose and that we could not do the alignment before replacing them. The customer started yelling, "Why should I pay $39.00! You didn't do anything!" Didn't do anything? Really? Altogether, we spent approximately thirty minutes inspecting and test driving his truck. In addition, we advised him on the condition of the ball joints and gave an estimate for repairs. But there was no pleasing him, he wanted to get something for nothing.

There is a very old saying that goes, "The laborer is worthy of his hire." It is good to be reminded of this from time to time. We as a society sometimes tend to want to get something for nothing, when in reality everybody who works or provides a service should be compensated for his or her labors or skills that they provide. However, this only applies to those services that both parties agree to. If you take your car to a repair shop for a headlight replacement, they have no right to charge you for a brake inspection or anything else that you didn't agree to.

Again, I can't stress enough the importance of good communication with your tech or service writer. In the beginning of Chapter 5, I mentioned that they will ask you some basic questions concerning what your car or truck is doing or not doing. Be as accurate and persistent as is necessary to get both of you on the same page. Was that noise you heard a squeak, a squeal, a squawk, a growl or a grind? It makes a difference to the technician who will be working on your vehicle. When it comes to a problem, don't tell them what you need or try to diagnose the problem for them. They are the experts, give them the information or data and let them diagnose the problem. Telling them that you need a four-wheel alignment when you actually need your tires balanced is a sure fire-way of having to make second trip to the repair shop to get the real problem corrected. These are real life scenarios that happen every day, at any given repair facility; mistakes like these will cost you time and money in the end.

Breaking Down the Parts of Your Estimate and Invoice

Now let's quickly talk a little bit about the parts of the estimate and the final bill, or invoice, that makes up the total dollar amount that you will pay when you pick up your vehicle. Estimates and more importantly the invoice will have a breakdown of the parts and labor costs. These make up the major portion of the estimate. Depending on your location, certain taxes may also be applied to the cost of the parts and labor. The total tax should be listed separately. Some locations may tax labor charges and others may not. On some work orders you may also see a category for shop supplies. This can be calculated in different ways but is usually based on a small percentage of the total work order excluding taxes. Some shops may factor the cost of shop supplies into the final bill by adding it to the parts cost. It is my belief, however, that it is better if everything is listed separately. That way the customer knows exactly how much they are paying for parts, labor, shop supplies and tax.

Quite often we are asked just what are the shop supplies for. These supplies include cleaners, grease, some topping off fluids, penetrating oils, and shop towels or any chemicals or adhesives needed to complete the job. It may also cover some nuts, bolts or other fasteners. Shop supplies is a fee that is spread across all of the work orders. Some use a lot of shop supplies and some require little, but everybody pays for the supplies required to make repairs, one way or another.

Parts Are Parts, Right?

At times, we may quote a specific repair and occasionally we may hear from the customer, "We can get that part a lot cheaper at XYZ Discount Auto Parts Store." Many think that parts are parts: it makes no difference where they come from so why not get the cheapest part available? With the deluge of discount auto parts commercials it's easy to fall into that cheapest part trap. Sometimes that discount store brand can be a half or even one-third of the cost of the brand name or factory part. As a seasoned technician, there is a huge difference! Now this debate may go on and on, but those of us who work in the industry, who have had to replace parts under warranty because of their inferior quality, know that there is a difference in sourced parts.

Along with the "lowest price in town" motto, many of these discount parts stores will also give the ever-popular "Lifetime guarantee!" Beware of these parts stores that offer you the world and want little in return: they sell volume. So, if a $19.95 part is returned after being installed for six to twelve months, they just replace the part and move on. However, many shops will only warranty the labor for twelve months and if a customer demands the use of a "more affordable" part won't warranty the labor at all, and here is why.

We once had a customer who needed the water pump replaced on their car. It was a very labor-intensive water pump to replace; there was a lot of tear down and reassembly on the front of the engine to the tune of approximately $600. We quoted the more expensive brand of water pump that had a proven track record. However, the customer demanded the cheaper pump, which saved him about

$50. After about fourteen months, the pump failed and this customer wanted us to replace it under full warranty. We declined to do so, stating that because the part had a "limited lifetime warranty" the parts store and our shop would honor that portion of the warranty, and not charge him for the replacement water pump. However, because they went against our recommendation, we could not cover the labor portion of the job. In short, saving himself $50 cost him much more in the end.

Now the moral of this story is simple: don't skimp on parts, especially when labor-intensive repairs are involved. It is better to pay a few extra dollars, get the good stuff, and not have to worry about having the same job redone any time soon. So if your tech offers you a $60 store brand wheel bearing or a $150 brand name bearing like Timken or Moog, go with the brand name if you can afford it. Also remember, when you are given an estimate for repairs, it is perfectly okay to ask the shop what type of parts they are installing: good quality factory or national brand parts or cheaper parts. Again, be informed! If you're spending hundreds or even thousands of your hard-earned dollars on a repair, insist on the good stuff!

When talking to seasoned techs either directly or perhaps through a message board on Identifix, it doesn't take long to discover that factory parts are the highest quality and on the top of the parts chain. But what if a factory part is not available or is obsolete, what then? Here is a pretty good rule of thumb that I use when advising my customers. It's fairly simple, keeps your newer car running like new, and saves you a little money on your older ride. Ah yes, we all want to save money.

In a nutshell, base the grade of part that is to be installed on your vehicle on its current condition and how much life that you and your tech thinks it has before going to that big scrapyard in the sky. That's it! I told you that it was simple. Okay, let me expound on this a little more.

Most of the vehicles engineered and built today have an excellent life expectancy if maintained properly. When you purchase a new car, while under warranty, it will be getting factory parts for any warranted repairs. Therefore, for the first three to six years, depending on the manufacturer and the warranty program, your vehicle will be getting those factory parts installed for warranted repairs. Now after the factory warranty period has expired is where you'll have the most important decisions to make regarding the parts that your tech will be installing on your vehicle.

As I mentioned, on your repair invoice the two areas that carry the most weight in terms of dollars and cents are parts and labor. That being said, the parts that you choose can possibly help maintain your vehicle in a "like new" condition or allow it to deteriorate into something that once resembled a classy sedan or coupe. So after your factory warranty has expired, I recommend that you continue to have those factory parts installed when practical, or the top tier aftermarket parts (the national brands that I mentioned earlier). I and many other technicians have discovered that certain electronic parts like sensors, engine controlling devices, some alternators, etc. are best purchased from the vehicle manufacturer or the aftermarket store if they offer manufacturer recommended parts such as Delphi, Bosch, Denso, Motorcraft, etc.

I want to step back for one moment and once again stress the importance that your repair shop subscribes to Identifix. There are some vehicles that can be temperamental when it comes to aftermarket parts. Here is a case in point mentioned on the forum: a vehicle came in with an alternator that wasn't charging the battery properly. Technician A stated that he had replaced the alternator twice. Each time the replacement alternator was charging yet the battery light on the instrument cluster indicated that it wasn't. The final fix was to install a manufacturer recommended rebuilt alternator. Bam! Problem fixed. Technician B comments in the same thread, "Had the same problem, tried cheaper store brand alternators with the same result. Installed the factory recommended and original equipment Bosch alternator and the problem is gone." Technician C again reiterates the same problem and solution. Without Identifix a tech can go off into left field trying to trouble-shoot a problem that isn't there thinking to themselves, "I just installed a new alternator, another problem must lie elsewhere." It is said, "Among a multitude of counselors there is safety." I would add, "And money saving opportunities!"

Now please don't misunderstand me on this point, I'm not saying that all aftermarket or store brand parts are bad. In fact, most of the time they will be fine. What I am saying is that certain vehicles require factory parts for the <u>most favorable and long-lasting</u> repair. So on a newer vehicle that you plan to keep for a long time, let's fix it right and forget it.

For suspension, steering, exhaust and brake parts, top tier aftermarket parts will usually serve you well and last as long as their factory counterpart lasts. I have also found that although store brand or aftermarket parts like power steering hoses, transmission cooler hoses and radiators may function properly, they may not fit correctly, causing more grief for your tech and possibly forcing them to make "modifications" to the new part or to your vehicle to get them to fit correctly. Factory parts are, for the most part, plug and play, meaning they fit almost perfectly because they are close if not exactly like the part that came out of your vehicle.

Okay, back to my original question. What if the manufacturers "factory" part is not available or obsolete? Then go to your second choice, the top tier aftermarket part. This is especially true when dealing with electronic parts.

Now, most aftermarket parts stores carry an "economy" line of parts. If you plan on keeping your vehicle for a few years then I would not recommend that these parts get installed on your vehicle because most likely they will need to be replaced again and perhaps again. Sometimes these economy parts don't give the expected result, and result in a stiff ride or a less than quiet outcome. In my opinion, here is when these economy parts fit the bill. If you plan on getting rid of the vehicle soon and it is, shall we say, well used, then go ahead and have this lower tier part installed. If the goal is to keep it going for a few more months until you're done with college and saving for that dream car when starting your new career, then go with the economy line.

Before moving on I want to leave you with a little bit more information to help empower you in this decision-making process. If you have a good relationship with your shop or tech already, talk to them about the parts that are going into your vehicle. A good shop will provide for this. Yes the parts may be a little more expensive, but you'll be much happier with the outcome. Now, if you are still looking for that trusted shop, don't be afraid to talk to them about the parts that they are using in your car or truck. Some shops may use lower quality parts to be price competitive with their competition. More about that in a bit.

"We Don't Install Customer-supplied Parts"

With the cost of everything going up, some try saving money by going to the parts store themselves, buying the parts, and having a shop install them. If you have thought about this and you do find a shop that will install customer-supplied parts, don't expect anything other than your parts installed. Don't expect any kind of diagnosis, any support after the parts are installed or any warranty. With some shops, you may see an increased labor rate or charge for such a service—or not see it and still be charged it. If the shop doesn't outwardly say that there is an increased labor charge, it may be hidden in the labor quote.

There is a cost of doing business that the repair shops have to consider when figuring labor rates and pricing parts. With most legitimate shops, parts are usually marked up approximately 40% to 60%. Okay, sit back and get it out of your system. This is a sore spot for many consumers when they can go get their parts at a discount auto parts store for a third of the price. This along with the labor rate is what is necessary to keep the shop doors open each month. It takes thousands of dollars each month to continue operating and serving customers. This goes towards education, updating and replacing tools, insurances, shop upkeep, advertising, warranties, payroll, etc. Without the profit from part sales, most shop labor rates would be astronomical or the shop owners would not be able to remain in business. Therefore, the mark-up on parts is just a part of the repair world. So if a shop agrees to install a part that you have purchased, understand that they will most likely increase the labor charge or decrease services in some way, and be aware of this when entering into this type of agreement.

In addition, many shops have signs stating, "We do not install customer-supplied parts." This avoids any misunderstanding and conflict with the customer if: 1) The customer provides the wrong part; 2) The customer supplies a defective or an inferior part; 3) A "hoist fee" is charged, which could become costly, if the vehicle sits disabled on a lift or hoist taking up valuable shop space waiting for the customer to correct #1 and #2. To eliminate the headaches associated with this scenario, let the shop quote the job using the parts that they recommend or that the two of you have discussed. It is my experience that in the end, customers who bring in their own parts don't usually save anything and at times it will actually cost them more. Some vehicles have many options that affect the correct part selection. If there are four options, sizes or configurations for a particular part on your vehicle, will you know which one it is?

Labor

Labor charges are composed of several factors. Most repair shops use some sort of a "flat rate" guide to determine labor charges for any given repair, and this is the starting point. I say that it is a starting point because your tech must calculate any additional time the job may require as the result of age, corrosion or present condition. For instance, if a guide says it takes three hours to remove the fuel tank, and replaced the fuel pump on a particular vehicle, this is assuming there is no corrosion and fuel lines that will break. If the vehicle is fifteen or twenty years old, and in an area of the country that uses a lot of salt in the winter time, there will most likely be corrosion build-up, making it much more difficult to replace the fuel pump. In this instance, depending on the severity of the corrosion and condition of the parts, an additional 20% to 50% may be added to the labor costs when quoted in the estimate.

Corroded, seized or broken hoses or lines, aftermarket accessories and diagnostic time all affect the labor portion of the estimate. This is not the fault of the shop or your technician, so remember that a flat rate guide is just that, a guide, and your technician is not constrained by it.

During diagnostic nightmares, if asked for "technical support" costs approval, I recommend that you give it to them. When your tech needs to consult with a tech support expert, it doesn't mean that they are incompetent, it just means that they know where to go for help and want to save money in the long run. They know when to get help to speed things along. In some cases an Identifix tech support call can have an additional cost associated with it, typically of around fifty dollars. Don't forget: if you decline a repair, you are still responsible for paying the diagnostic charges.

Apples to Apples

Many new customers like to price shop and get the best deal possible. This is very prudent when a long-term working relationship with a shop has not yet been established. When price shopping however, make sure that you are comparing apples to apples.

As I mentioned in the previous paragraphs, there is a lot that goes into an estimate and there can be a wide range between shops when it comes to parts and labor charges. If you decide to call a shop for an estimate, they should take the time to look up the parts and labor for that particular job that you are requesting. If they begin throwing numbers at you without looking anything up then beware, especially if they are significantly lower than other shops. Cheaper isn't always better. This is a further reason why it's very important that you build a good and long-lasting relationship with a reputable shop, who will treat you fairly and consistently.

"My neighbor can do that!" If I had a dollar every time I heard that or a variation on it (my brother, spouse, etc.), I would be a wealthy man. I'm not trying to insult you or your family or friends—that is the last thing that I want to do here—but let's face it, we all should know our limitations and those of our loved ones. Now, the point that I'm trying to make is this, even though a family member or friend can "fix the broken wire," should they? I once had a customer who after receiving my estimate for a drum brake repair promptly stated, "Oh, my husband can do that…" A week later, the vehicle was towed to my shop with a box of brake parts sitting on the passenger's seat. The poor guy couldn't figure out how all of those pieces and parts (those that weren't missing) went back together. I can drywall a room for you, but you wouldn't want me to… Don't base the price you're willing to pay for a repair on what a family member or friend tells you they would do it for.

Another point I would like to make is this: there is a risk when requesting a quote for a repair to a problem that someone else has diagnosed. Remember, Uncle George may have had good intentions when he sent you down for that light-bulb, but sometimes it can get frightful when a shop just replaces a part or makes a repair based on someone else's diagnosis. Just because your physician says you need to have surgery doesn't make it so. In most cases, you will see a surgeon to verify your doctor's findings first. In the same way, have your technician diagnose or verify any findings that Uncle George (or for that matter another repair shop) found before making a repair or replacing a part.

There is a reverse side of this that can create a great deal of grief as well. If your tech diagnoses a problem, it is preferable to let them make the repair. Countless times, I've seen situations where a tech will diagnose a problem and the customer, not wanting to pay for the repair, decides to do the repair him or herself. Unless they have the necessary skills and the correct tools to do the repair, this is not recommended. Here is another example that occurred a few years ago. A new customer had their car towed to the shop; the vehicle had died while driving. We had diagnosed a faulty ignition module and quoted the repair accordingly. Thinking they would save themselves money, they had the vehicle towed home so that they could do the repair. A few days later, they called, expressing their dissatisfaction that the ignition module "didn't fix the problem!" We were not able to help them at that point. They may have used a faulty or inferior part, or they may have installed it incorrectly. There's no way of knowing because they refused to return it for us to complete the repair. If we had done the repair, they would have driven off with a parts and labor warranty.

The particular point that I'm making is this: when price shopping and getting the best deal, make sure you are comparing apples to apples. Are the different shops that you are requesting quotes from using the same parts? What kind of warranty do each of them provide, if any? Do all of the quotes include diagnosis and repairs? Don't forget to compare the labor rates. If a quote or estimate comes in much lower or higher than the others, find out why, ask questions; there may be a very good reason why the estimates are so far apart. Don't just assume that the repair shops with the highest estimates are over-charging.

"I Didn't Build It, I Didn't Buy It and I Didn't Break It"

When a customer's vehicle has been diagnosed and the repair estimate completed, it's the job of the service writer or technician to call you with the good or not so good news. Unfortunately, at times, these two individuals are the recipients of some pretty harsh comments from the owners of the vehicles. It's good to remember that when you hire a shop to repair your car or truck, you didn't hire them to make you feel good or give you warm fuzzies inside. Although we all want to give our customers good news, technicians are there for one purpose: to diagnose and repair your vehicle. It's not the fault of the shop or technician if a customer doesn't have enough money to repair their car, and this is where most of the animosity stems from: lack of funds for the repair.

Chapter 2 is where I recommended that everyone save up $500 to $1,500 and keep it available for automotive repairs. This is why, for those unexpected repairs that WILL arise. When the repair fund is empty, the news from your service writer or tech will be a major bump in the road. In addition, that is when the news that they give you may be intolerable. The shop is full of witty little sayings, and here is another that techs may convey to a difficult customer: "I didn't build it, I didn't buy it and I didn't break it."

Know Your Rights

Many inexperienced consumers either don't know or forget that they have certain rights when working with repair shops and it's good to keep these in mind, especially during the initial phases of building that long-term relationship. During this critical time, it is important that you get involved with the repair process of your vehicle. I don't mean by picking up a wrench and getting dirty. I'm talking about getting involved, being informed before making any approval decisions. A less than trustworthy repair shop has the advantage because they are relying on the customer's lack of knowledge and not taking the time to check up on them and what they are doing.

Okay, I'm not trying to paint a bleak picture of the automotive repair industry, but as with any other service and retail trade, it is in the best interests of the consumer to research and follow up before committing. Again, as this relationship is developed there is a certain amount of trust that is built between the two parties. Until then, here is what you can do to be more involved.

During the diagnostic and estimating process, request a price breakdown. Instead of grouping parts or procedures under a single heading, ask them to itemize the repair. Ask your tech to write <u>why</u> they replaced the wheel bearing. Was it to correct an ABS problem? Was it loose or noisy?

The invoice should list the symptom and the steps to correct the problem and the parts used. Which is more informative and helps to explain what you are paying $300 for: "Replaced wheel bearing" or "Test drove vehicle, heard slightly excessive wheel bearing noise coming from the left front, inspected bearings for looseness, all bearings feel tight at this time. Ran diagnostic tests, found chassis module code C0035 stored, checked resistance in left front wheel speed sensor circuit and found high resistance in sensor. Replaced left front wheel bearing; vehicle has high mileage on it and the bearing was noisy. The wheel speed sensor is an integral part of the wheel bearing. Cleared code and test drove vehicle, bearing noise is gone and the code did not return"? Now the two examples are opposite extremes used to make a point. Instead of just blindly paying $300 for a repair, get some evidence that the problem was diagnosed and repaired correctly and that you won't be returning in a few days because the problem was never corrected.

If you have questions about what the shop is doing, you have the right to ask to see what the problem is. This may be an inconvenience to you if you are not sitting in the waiting room. Nevertheless you can request to be shown where the problem(s) lie. If you are not on site, you'll need to go right down to the shop so as not to hold them up, tying up valuable shop floor space, but most shops will accommodate their customers who would like to see what the problem is.

Another way that you can get involved is to ask to see your old parts when it's time to pick up your car or truck. If you wish, you can also request to get your old parts back and take them with you, as long as there is no core charge involved. If the part has a deposit or "core" charge then it is best just to look at it and let the shop keep it so that they can return it to the parts store for the credit. If a customer wishes to take the part with them then the core charge will be added to their bill. Sometimes this is necessary if a customer installed a part themselves that has failed and they want to return it to the store for a refund or credit. Many states require that auto repair shops make the replaced parts available to the consumer as proof that the part in question was actually replaced. Yes, unfortunately some unscrupulous shops may say that they replaced a given part when they never did. Sad face…

Don't Keep Paying for the "Same" Repair

We discussed earlier what goes into the making of a reputable repair shop. To recap or reiterate, a good shop invests a lot of time, money and training to ensure that their customer's vehicle is repaired right the first time; or, in the case of intermittent problems, communicates with their customers their best and most cost-effective options.

Not all shops are that dedicated, however. In this case, there are times when a customer will keep paying for the same repair as the repair shop continues to "replace" different parts. If this has been your experience, and you know what I'm talking about, then you need to bail out and find a different repair facility. You need a shop that will actually diagnose the problem, not just throw parts at it with the hopes that one of them will fix the problem. At times there will be a judgment call on your part, as with the example I gave of the customer who needed the power steering gear and hoses replaced. It took several return trips to get a bad repair job corrected. They wanted to give up on the other shop and have us do the repair all over again, but with our recommendations, this customer stayed persistent and finally got the job corrected at no additional costs to themselves.

Patience Is a Virtue

We live our lives at a much faster pace than our grandparents, or even our parents for some of us. It's been said that our world has become a world of instant gratification and instant results. The *"I want it now!"* syndrome has taken over to some degree or another. This is no different when it comes to our vehicles, so many of us don't set ourselves up for the possibility of being without them for a few of days. Today, our vehicles are so reliable that we don't give it a second thought, just start the engine and off we go. Nevertheless, what happens in the event that you are suddenly without your car or truck for a few days? This is when patience with your repair shop comes into play.

On about a weekly basis, a version of the following happens. Perhaps some of the details are a little different, but overall there is the same cause and the same end result. A car gets towed in or is dropped off the night before by the owner. The shop opens up the next morning at 8:00 am, and by 9:00 or 10:00 the customer is calling to see if their car is done yet, and if not, how long will it take.

"You can have a good job, a fast job or a cheap job. Pick any two." We read this and chuckle a bit, but think about it for a moment. In the service industry, rarely can we get all three at the same time; sometimes circumstances beyond our control will affect the speed, accuracy and cost of a service or repair. Again, for the best result that will save you money, being patient will serve you best in the end.

Now I'm not talking about the shop that tells you that they will be getting your car into the shop next, and two weeks later it's still sitting out in the parking lot. That's when you should hold them accountable, know your rights and have it towed to another shop if necessary. What I am talking about is giving your repair shop a reasonable amount of time to complete the diagnosis and repair process. A good repair facility will stay in touch with you and keep you in the loop. We once had a customer who would call us every thirty minutes or so for a status update on a major engine repair. We advised him that there was no update yet, and kindly told him that all the frequent calling was doing was interrupting his technician's concentration during a very critical moment and slowing down the repair. Thankfully, with the advent of caller I.D., we stopped answering the phone and called him with status updates when practical.

So the moral of this particular story is this: for the best result, give your tech some time to diagnose your vehicle's problem or get the repair completed. Although you may be a little anxious, it's best not to interrupt or rush the surgeon. Some repairs are not so cut and dried, and take time to complete. Yet if you connect with a good repair shop, they will keep you updated on the repair process and won't leave you in the dark.

What About Insurance Related Repairs?

The repair process can take a little longer for any repair jobs that involve insurance companies, for example a vehicle that was caught in flood waters or perhaps slid into a curb. To expedite the process, it is advisable that you, the owner of the vehicle stay involved. Don't assume that your regular repair facility will take care of everything and handle the insurance claim on your behalf; many smaller shops aren't set up to be the intermediary for an insurance claim. If this is the case, then the shop may want you to pay for the repair and then the insurance company can reimburse you. Nevertheless, talk to your shop representative and see what they can do for you.

It is times like these that the line of communication breaks down and the vehicle will sit while the customer and the shop are waiting for each other to handle the insurance claim. Not only does this postpone the owner getting their car back, some shops may even charge a storage fee if it is left sitting on their lot for an excessive amount of time. You, your repair shop and the insurance company should stay in contact with each other if you find yourself in an insurance claim situation. The sooner the insurance adjuster comes out and inspects your vehicle, the sooner the repairs can begin. The repair shop won't begin any work until the dollar amount for the repair has been agreed upon between you, your insurance company and them.

If the insurance claim involves a fender bender, that will involve bodywork, and your best option is to take it directly to a body shop. Many times a vehicle that has been in an accident will be driven or towed to an auto repair shop and then sit for a few days before the insurance claim adjuster comes out to inspect the vehicle. At that point, they may require that your vehicle go to an auto body shop for repairs. Even if the body damage is minimal, and your repair facility can do the suspension repairs, many insurance companies will want the vehicle to go to the body shop because their labor rates are generally a little lower than that of a mechanical repair shop. That being said, if suspension work needs to be done, if you want your shop to do the repairs, the insurance company will pay a certain amount based on THEIR estimate and you will pay the balance of the bill based on your repair shop's estimate. Generally speaking, the insurance company's estimate will almost always be less than that of your repair facility. Because many auto body shops have a good working relationship with the insurance companies and their hourly rates tend to be lower, most of the time it is more advantageous, and more cost effective, to let those two parties handle the insurance related repairs.

Time to Pick Up Your Ride

So now you've received the phone call that repairs on your car are complete and it's ready to be picked up. You're excited that your ride is repaired and your life can now get back to normal. This is the final crucial step to make sure that you're getting what you paid for, nothing more and nothing less. Here is what to do.

Previously in this chapter I mentioned this, and I can't emphasize it enough: hold your repair shop accountable. Now is the time to look over and pay your invoice. Make sure you are paying for what you had agreed to. Read it carefully; are there any duplicate parts or labor charges? Sometimes, even with the best of care, mistakes happen, so it's up to you to give your invoice a final scrutinizing. Now is the time to request to see and inspect any old parts that they replaced, now is the time to take a quick look at your car or truck for any external damage, before you drive off their parking lot. Once you leave, the parts go into the trash or out for recycling and you may have no recourse if you find a dent in the fender or a broken tail-light. So don't be in a hurry: take some time to ask any final questions and inspect your vehicle before you get in and drive off.

If by chance you see any damage to your car while it was in the shop's possession, bring it to your shop's attention before leaving, take pictures and talk to them about it. It may not necessarily be their fault—another customer could have bumped into your vehicle. In any case, you and your shop will want to talk about whose insurance will cover the repairs depending on what happened or how the damage occurred. It is for this reason that an initial inspection of the exterior of your vehicle was so important when you dropped it off for repairs. Without it, it could turn into an ugly "he said, she said" scenario. Although it's rare that this happens, if by chance something is wrong (they broke/damaged something), have them make it right, hold them accountable.

Finally, yet importantly, test drive your car or truck. Did the repair shop correct the problem to your satisfaction? If so, when you get a chance, stop by and thank them for their expertise. This will go a long way on your next visit! If the problem with your vehicle is still present or it returns, as is sometimes the case with intermittent problems, call them or stop by as soon as possible, preferably within a day or two. Too often, a customer doesn't want to be inconvenienced, so they don't return, and then six months later they bring it to the shop's attention. Don't wait: get back in there and talk to them about it, perhaps have your tech go on another test drive with you. Sometimes repairs can be a process, and it may take a couple of visits to get all of your concerns addressed.

In this chapter, we've covered a lot of ground and material. Although this is easy for many, it can be distressing to the point of tears for others. As you will see, when a good working relationship is established with a trusted repair shop or dealership, the write-up and repair process is predictable and seamless.

Conclusion

Over the course of the last century, many aspects of our driving habits have changed, from the vehicles we get into, to the traffic laws that we are compelled to follow. The cars and trucks that we have the privilege of driving are far more advanced than those of our grandparent's or great-grandparent's generation. Our vehicles are truly an extension of ourselves. Many come with such luxuries as heated seats, satellite radio, computerized climate controlled systems and so much more! Driving and owning a vehicle can be an expensive venture in many aspects. On the other hand, driving today can be such an exhilarating experience if we prepare ourselves for it.

Over the course of the last seven chapters, we've talked about safety and our responsibility to others. We've also covered purchasing new and used vehicles, and what it takes to maintain them in a manner that won't break the bank. As with all relationships, the one that you build with your technician can be very beneficial to you and your family. My goal in writing this book is to help those in need. Over the past thirty-five years, I've seen hundreds of situations that could have been avoided if the consumers had been properly educated. I believe that these experiences and recommendations that I have shared with you will be a catalyst for a more positive driving experience.

Getting behind the wheel should be an enjoyable experience; I know it was for me back when I was driving my 1972 Volkswagen Beetle. Today I drive a 2016 Chevrolet Colorado; what a difference forty years has made! Whatever you drive, if you follow the recommendations outlined in this book, although I can't guarantee that you won't hit any bumps in the proverbial road, I can assure you that they will be fewer and further between! With that, to all of my fellow drivers out there behind the wheel and on the open road, drive on!

If you would like to learn more and perhaps share some your experiences or comment on our blog, go to our companion website www.gettingbehindthewheel.com.

What's that Mean?

Here is a list of some of the most common symptoms that we run across and what they may mean.

Drivability Symptoms

Check engine or Service Engine Soon (SES) light on: As I mentioned earlier in this book, there could be hundreds of causes for this condition. If you have a code reader/scan tool, like the BlueDriver, then scan for any current codes. This will help indicate the severity of the problem. Some faults are urgent and some not so much. Retrieve any codes and call your technician to determine your best course of action.

Rough running engine while sitting still and/or while accelerating: This may be due to a misfiring engine, in other words, not all of the engine's cylinders are working properly. Many times, if severe enough, the check engine or Service Engine Soon light may be flashing. Many things can cause this, including worn-out spark plugs, or an ignition coil or fuel injector that is not working properly. Low compression in one or more of the cylinders or a weak fuel pump can also cause this. Any number of sensors including the Crankshaft (CKP) or Camshaft (CMP) Position Sensor; Mass Air Flow (MAF) or Manifold Absolute Pressure (MAP) sensors can cause this condition. If this occurs, have your vehicle towed to your repair shop. Don't continue to drive your car or truck; further damage may be done to the engine if you do.

Idles okay and is smooth but lacks power under acceleration: The most common causes for this is a restriction somewhere in the air intake, exhaust or fuel systems. The air or fuel filters may be dirty or plugged; or there may be a catalytic converter that is restricted. If this condition progresses, or is bad enough, then the vehicle may no longer idle smoothly. If a brake caliper locks up (seizes) or the parking brake doesn't release, this too can give the sensation that the vehicle is lacking power. In truth, the vehicle may have plenty of power but is held back by the braking system. Again, don't continue to drive your car or truck in this condition, get it to your technician for repairs as soon as possible before further damage is done to your engine or braking system.

Engine overheating: This may be caused by a stuck thermostat, a restricted radiator or a cylinder head gasket that has failed; often it is said that the "head gasket is blown." When the engine is cool, check the coolant level. If the coolant level is low then there is a leak somewhere, either internally or externally. The vehicle should be towed to your repair shop if it is overheating so that your technician can do pressure tests to find any leaks. If the head gasket is suspected as being faulty, then they may want to do a Blue Water Test, which can often help detect exhaust gasses in the cooling system.

Rattling, grinding or squealing noise coming from under the hood: If one or more of these noises are heard whenever the engine is running, and may get worse the faster the engine is running, then there may be a problem with the accessory drive belt or one of the drive belt pulleys or tensioners. There may also be a problem with one of the accessories that are driven, like the alternator, water pump or air conditioner compressor. Get the vehicle to your technician before further damage is done.

Brakes and Exhaust Symptoms

Grinding noise while stopping at any speed: Many times this grinding sensation can be felt in the steering wheel or throughout the vehicle. This usually indicates that the brake pad material is completely diminished and the brake pad backing plate or shoe, which is made of metal, is now grinding against the brake rotor or drum, which is also made up of metal. Stop driving your vehicle and get it towed to your repair shop.

High-pitched tinny sounding squeal: This may happen when lightly braking, or you may hear is while turning at slower speeds. Most likely, this is the brake wear indicator rubbing on the brake rotor. It's time for a brake inspection and possible brake work done. If ignored for too long, it will turn into the grinding noise just mentioned.

High-pitched squeal while low speed braking: This is a squeal you may hear when coming to a stop, usually from lower speeds like 10 mph or less. Often it occurs when the brake pads and rotors are cold and many times the squeal will go away as the brakes warm up. This may be the squeal that is heard from glazing on the brake pads or shoes. When there are smooth, mirror like surfaces, rubbing against each other, this causes a high frequency vibration resulting in a squeal. Typically braking isn't affected and can be eliminated with resurfacing the pads and rotors.

Brake pedal pulsation and possible steering wheel vibration when braking: This pulsation is due to warped brake drums or rotors. If there is a brake pedal pulsation and a vibration is felt in the steering wheel, then the problem lies in the front brakes. If there is a brake pulsation with no steering wheel vibration, then the problem lies within the rear brake system. This is a general guideline, however. If the brake pulsation is bad enough, it may be necessary to correct the obvious problem, i.e. the front or rear brakes, first and then re-evaluate the problem to see if further brake work is necessary. In any event, replacing the affected drums or rotors along with a new set of brake pads or shoes with **high quality parts** will take care of this issue. It is a good idea to replace brake calipers that are old or not operating smoothly as this could be the root cause of one or more of the brake rotors warping in the first place.

High-pitched vibration coming from under the vehicle: This noise may be heard while sitting still and revving the engine slightly. In other words, while the vehicle is still in park and the accelerator pedal is "snapped" slightly (pressed and released quickly), a high-pitched vibration from under the vehicle may be heard. Often times this is an exhaust shield or exhaust component that has broken or become loose and is vibrating, causing that annoying sound. Check with your technician, he may be able to refasten any loose parts or advise you in any other repairs if it gets more involved.

Rattle in the rear of the vehicle while going over bumps: This may be a loose exhaust or broken exhaust hangers or components. This is not to be confused with suspension symptoms. Sometimes this sound may be compared to a "thudding" noise that the exhaust makes while banging on or against a chassis part or cross-member while going over bumps. This may also make a vibration sound that may be felt in the car while sitting still with the engine idling. If an exhaust hanger is broken, it is advisable to get your vehicle to your repair shop as soon as possible before further, more expensive, damage is done to the vehicle.

Wheels and Suspension Symptoms

Uneven wear patterns on the tires: The vehicle's four wheels not being in proper alignment will cause this, and the vehicle may also pull to the left or right. To correct this condition, the vehicle may simply require a re-alignment of the wheels. However, in many cases the root cause for the alignment to go out in the first place may be worn or bent suspension parts. Worn ball joints, tie rods, shocks or struts, wheel bearings can all cause uneven tire wear. If the vehicle has hit a curb or pothole at a higher speed, suspension parts could be bent. Get the vehicle to your repair shop: suspension parts will most likely need to be replaced and a wheel alignment completed to correct this.

A single popping noise when starting or coming to a stop: Sometimes this can be felt as well as heard; many times is could be a loose or worn ball joint. A control arm that has a worn bushing can cause this noise as well and may give the sensation that something is shifting when coming to a stop at slow speeds. This can be verified by having a friend stand to either side, and then watching the front wheels when coming to a stop. If the wheels shift to the rear, then the lower control arm bushings will be in order. It is most cost effective to have the whole control arm replaced as a unit because then the bushing(s), control arm and ball joint are replaced at the same time without any additional labor charges.

Higher frequency rattling sound coming from the front or rear of the vehicle while going over small bumps at slower speeds: This is usually an indication of a worn sway bar (stabilizer bar) control link(s). Although it is very annoying, it is not an emergency. Get your vehicle to your tech as soon as possible so that he or she can confirm the diagnosis. Excessive tire wear and vehicle stability concerns will be the result if ignored.

Deeper pitched rattle, almost a knocking or "thudding" noise while going over bumps or potholes: This may sound a little different from the sound that worn sway bar links make. Worn struts or strut bushings are a common cause for this. Some vehicles can make this similar sound when the sway bar mounting bushings are worn or dry. However, it's best not to guess; many have replaced the struts (not cheap) to find out that the sway bar mounting bushings were worn or dry. After lubricating or replacing the bushings, a relatively inexpensive fix, the noise went away.

A "whirring" noise that intensifies with speed: This is usually a wheel bearing that has gone or is going bad. It may intensify while turning at higher speeds, like abruptly going from one lane to another. Often it can be compared to the sound that a propeller airplane makes. As with a propeller, the faster it spins, the louder the "whirring" sound gets. The faster a worn wheel bearing goes, the louder this "whirring" noise gets. It is best to get the vehicle to your repair shop as soon as possible, if left unchecked further damage can occur.

With each of the listed symptoms that I've mentioned, or if anything else about your vehicle doesn't quite seem normal, it is highly recommended that the vehicle be taken to your trusted service technician so that they can advise you.

Throughout this book I've talked about ways to save money. Here I would like to leave you with these two reminders. Don't let anyone "Easter Egg" to find your vehicle's problem. In other words, it can get very expensive trying this part or that part hoping to fix the problem. Moreover, as I mentioned, many times multiple problems can have the same symptom. A small repair can turn into a huge, very expensive repair because the vehicle owner procrastinated to the point that the vehicle was no longer drivable. Therefore, as soon as your car or truck exhibits any of these symptoms, get it to your tech and save yourself the headache of a tow bill and possibly a more expensive repair bill. An ounce of prevention is truly worth a pound of cure!

Websites to Remember

www.gettingbehindthewheel.com
www.textinganddrivingsafety.com
www.carfax.com
www.kbb.com
www.nadaguides.com
www.carcarekiosk.com
www.fueleconomy.gov
www.asashop.org
www.ase.com
www.bbb.org
www.api.org
www.lemurmonitors.com
www.obd-codes.com
www.auto-dictionary.com

Made in the USA
Columbia, SC
06 December 2017